PSYCHOLOGY OF EMOTIONS, MOTIVATIONS AND ACTIONS

PSYCHOLOGY OF HABITS

PSYCHOLOGY OF EMOTIONS, MOTIVATIONS AND ACTIONS

Additional books in this series can be found on Nova's website under the Series tab.

Additional e-books in this series can be found on Nova's website under the e-book tab.

PSYCHOLOGY OF EMOTIONS, MOTIVATIONS AND ACTIONS

PSYCHOLOGY OF HABITS

ROBIN MAZZARIELLO
EDITOR

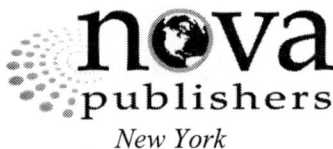

nova
publishers

New York

NOTICE TO THE READER

The Publisher has taken reasonable care in the preparation of this book, but makes no expressed or implied warranty of any kind and assumes no responsibility for any errors or omissions. No liability is assumed for incidental or consequential damages in connection with or arising out of information contained in this book. The Publisher shall not be liable for any special, consequential, or exemplary damages resulting, in whole or in part, from the readers' use of, or reliance upon, this material. Any parts of this book based on government reports are so indicated and copyright is claimed for those parts to the extent applicable to compilations of such works.

Independent verification should be sought for any data, advice or recommendations contained in this book. In addition, no responsibility is assumed by the publisher for any injury and/or damage to persons or property arising from any methods, products, instructions, ideas or otherwise contained in this publication.

This publication is designed to provide accurate and authoritative information with regard to the subject matter covered herein. It is sold with the clear understanding that the Publisher is not engaged in rendering legal or any other professional services. If legal or any other expert assistance is required, the services of a competent person should be sought. FROM A DECLARATION OF PARTICIPANTS JOINTLY ADOPTED BY A COMMITTEE OF THE AMERICAN BAR ASSOCIATION AND A COMMITTEE OF PUBLISHERS.

Additional color graphics may be available in the e-book version of this book.

Library of Congress Cataloging-in-Publication Data

Psychology of habits / editor, Robin Mazzariello. pages cm
Includes index.
ISBN: 978-1-62948-959-9 (soft cover)
1. Food habits--Psychology. 2. Eating disorders. I. Mazzariello, Robin.
TX357.P89 2014
394.1'2--dc23

                              2013048327

Published by Nova Science Publishers, Inc. † *New York*

CONTENTS

PREFACE

An important consideration in clinical nutrition management is food habits. The psychology of food habits is very interesting and can be useful for management of nutritional problems. Specific eating habits are accompanied by changes in patient's own body perception, psychological well-being and interpersonal relationships. The dissatisfaction with one's own appearance and the pursuit to reduce body mass start to be in the center of patient's attention which may result in various psycho-pathological symptoms. This book focuses on the psychological wellbeing and attitude towards one's own sexuality in female users of Polish websites on eating disorders; Sleep, television, texting and computer habits in schoolchildren and adolescents that are overweight; the psychology of food habits in an Indochina context; and the disordered eating habits among adolescents.

Chapter 1 – Introduction: A growing number of people are suffering from eating disorders. At the same time, the average age of incidence in case of eating disorders is becoming lower. Specific eating habits are accompanied by changes in patient's own body perception, psychological well-being and interpersonal relationships. The dissatisfaction with one's own appearance and the pursuit to reduce body mass start to be in the center of patient's attention which may result in various psycho-pathological symptoms. Nowadays, the cyberspace becomes a ground for the exchange of experiences connected with one's health and mental and physical state, offering thematic websites, forums and blogs. The aim of the research was to evaluate chosen aspects of emotional state (i.e., mood, the presence of depression, emotional aspects of sexuality) in the users of Polish websites on eating disorders. Material and method: 14 Polish websites connected with the topic of eating disorders were featuring a link to a website created for the sake of this research for the period of 2 months. The website included: information about the research, instructions and four questionnaires (i.e., Emotional State Questionnaire, Beck Depression Inventory (BDI), Multidimensional Sexuality Self-Concept Questionnaire (MSSCQ) and an original survey form). Full set of tools was filled in by 200 girls and women aged between 10 and 35. The average age of the respondents was 20.21±2,14. The majority of respondents lived in a city, were single and their body mass was normal. Results: The majority of respondents do not accept their bodies (78.5%), are afraid of putting on weight (86.5%), persistently think about food (76.5%) and their body mass (86%) and feel guilty about eating (75%). 72.5% of the respondents admit that their physical and psychological state is dependent of their body mass. Because of their current body mass the respondents experience low mood (79%) and suicidal ideation (51%). The majority of respondents present syndromes of depression (93%) varying in terms of their intensity. 69.5% of the respondents are currently on a slimming diet, whereas 55% visit websites on eating disorders more than once a week. The data analysis conducted with the use of STATISTICA software package has shown differences in the level of depression in patients which varied according to: the frequency of thinking about one's body mass ($p<0.001$), the frequency of visiting webpages on eating disorders ($p<0.001$) and the duration of a diet (0.01). Moreover, the research has revealed a difference in the sense of control over one's sexuality depending on the assessment of one's own body ($p<0.05$). However, the relations between being on a slimming diet and having the feeling of psychological benefit, motivation for having sex and feeling afraid of having sex and sexual relationships have not been proven in the research. Conclusions: Female users of websites on eating disorders do not accept their own bodies which is connected with focusing on one's appearance and having low mood and low control over one's sexuality. Possibly, at least a part of the users fulfill the diagnostic criteria of eating disorders.

Chapter 2 – This chapter provides a synthesis of three earlier published studies (Garmy et al. 2012[a]; Garmy et al. 2012[b]; Garmy et al. 2013) (survey I) as well as previously unpublished results from a survey conducted in 2013 among students aged 16 (survey II). Objective: The aim was to investigate the effects of sleep, television use and texting and computer habits on overweight, enjoyment of school and feelings of tiredness at school in school-age children and adolescents. Methods: This cross-sectional study was conducted in Sweden on schoolchildren aged 6, 7, 10, 14 and 16. A questionnaire which had been satisfactorily tested for validity and reliability was distributed to the children (n=3011 in survey I; n=204 in survey II). Results: Children who slept less than the median length of time reported enjoying school to a lesser degree. Fewer hours of sleep were found to be associated with having a bedroom television, using the television or computer more than 2 hours a day, being tired at school, and having difficulties in sleeping and waking up. Overweight and obesity were found in 15.8% of the study population; obesity alone was found in 3.1%. Relationships between lifestyle factors and overweight were studied using multivariate logistic regression analysis. Having a bedroom television and using the television more than 2 hours per day were found to be associated with overweight, but using the computer more than 2 hours a day was not. About 61% of the students aged 16 reported checking Facebook or social media at least once a day, and 27% reported doing so more than 10 times a day. One fourth of the students aged 16 had a habit of sending or receiving text messages at night at least once a week. Texting at night and frequent checking of Facebook and social media sites were related to sleep problems. *Conclusions:* Educating schoolchildren and their parents regarding matters of optimal sleep and how media habits affect sleep, overweight and learning is considered an important task.

Chapter 3 – An important consideration in clinical nutrition management is food habits. The psychology of food habits is very interesting and can be useful for management of nutritional problem. Sometimes, the spiritual aspect of food habits play important role as determinant of final overt food habits. The holy food habits must be well explored and understood by practitioner. The important habits on holy feast and holy fast are the general appearances in many communities, especially those in developing countries. In this article, the authors briefly review and discuss on Psychology of holy food habits, feast and fast, in Indochina, a developing region of the world at present, context.

Chapter 4 – Disordered eating habits among adolescents remains a major global problem that can affect their physical, mental and behavioral development. In spite of the advances that have been made in feeding practices, adolescents in many environments consume diets that are nutritionally inadequate, in that they do not provide adequate amounts of essential nutrients. Adolescence is a period which is critical and characterized by various growth spurts. Some of these growth spurts are psychological and emotional. Good dietary habits have also been found to be crucial in the development and growth of the adolescent during these periods. These psychological and emotional changes can lead to eating disorders if not well attended to. The three main types of disordered eating habits that can affect adolescents are anorexia nervosa, bulimia nervosa and binge eating disorder. In this review the use of a multidisciplinary approach in ensuring optimum adolescent growth was addressed. This approach included the use of parents/care-takers, teachers, dieticians, clinical psychologists and counsellors to ensure healthy eating habits of some adolescents. The results indicated the invaluable contribution of all the stakeholders in achieving good nutrition among adolescents.

In: Psychology of Habits
Editor: Robin Mazzariello

ISBN: 978-1-62948-959-9
© 2014 Nova Science Publishers, Inc.

Chapter 1

PSYCHOLOGICAL WELLBEING AND ATTITUDE TOWARDS ONE'S OWN SEXUALITY IN FEMALE USERS OF POLISH WEBSITES ON EATING DISORDERS

Monika Bąk-Sosnowska[1,*], *Katarzyna Potempa*[2] *and Mateusz Warchał*[3]

[1]Department of Psychology, Faculty of Health Sciences,
Medical University of Silesia, Katowice, Poland,
[2]Health Care Team, Wadowice, Poland
[3]Department of Social Factors and Methodology,
Institute of Occupational Medicine and Environmental Health,
Sosnowiec, Poland

ABSTRACT

Introduction: A growing number of people are suffering from eating disorders. At the same time, the average age of incidence in case of eating disorders is becoming lower. Specific eating habits are accompanied by changes in patient's own body perception, psychological well-being and interpersonal relationships. The dissatisfaction with one's own

[*] Corresponding author: Monika Bąk-Sosnowska, Department of Psychology, Faculty of Health Sciences, Medical University of Silesia, Medyków Street 12, 40-752 Katowice, Poland, tel / fax +48 32 208 86 42, e-mail: b_monique@poczta.onet.pl.

appearance and the pursuit to reduce body mass start to be in the center of patient's attention which may result in various psycho-pathological symptoms. Nowadays, the cyberspace becomes a ground for the exchange of experiences connected with one's health and mental and physical state, offering thematic websites, forums and blogs. The aim of the research was to evaluate chosen aspects of emotional state (i.e., mood, the presence of depression, emotional aspects of sexuality) in the users of Polish websites on eating disorders.

Material and method: 14 Polish websites connected with the topic of eating disorders were featuring a link to a website created for the sake of this research for the period of 2 months. The website included: information about the research, instructions and four questionnaires (i.e., Emotional State Questionnaire, Beck Depression Inventory (BDI), Multidimensional Sexuality Self-Concept Questionnaire (MSSCQ) and an original survey form). Full set of tools was filled in by 200 girls and women aged between 10 and 35. The average age of the respondents was $20.21\pm2,14$. The majority of respondents lived in a city, were single and their body mass was normal.

Results: The majority of respondents do not accept their bodies (78.5%), are afraid of putting on weight (86.5%), persistently think about food (76.5%) and their body mass (86%) and feel guilty about eating (75%). 72.5% of the respondents admit that their physical and psychological state is dependent of their body mass. Because of their current body mass the respondents experience low mood (79%) and suicidal ideation (51%). The majority of respondents present syndromes of depression (93%) varying in terms of their intensity. 69.5% of the respondents are currently on a slimming diet, whereas 55% visit websites on eating disorders more than once a week. The data analysis conducted with the use of STATISTICA software package has shown differences in the level of depression in patients which varied according to: the frequency of thinking about one's body mass ($p<0.001$), the frequency of visiting webpages on eating disorders ($p<0.001$) and the duration of a diet (0.01). Moreover, the research has revealed a difference in the sense of control over one's sexuality depending on the assessment of one's own body ($p<0.05$). However, the relations between being on a slimming diet and having the feeling of psychological benefit, motivation for having sex and feeling afraid of having sex and sexual relationships have not been proven in the research.

Conclusions: Female users of websites on eating disorders do not accept their own bodies which is connected with focusing on one's appearance and having low mood and low control over one's sexuality. Possibly, at least a part of the users fulfill the diagnostic criteria of eating disorders.

INTRODUCTION

Eating disorders are defined by abnormal eating habits or behavior involving body mass control. In current Diagnostic and Statistical Manual of Mental Disorders (5th Edition: DSM-V) the following classifications of feeding and eating disorders can be found (APA, 2013): pica, rumination syndrome (RS), binge eating disorder (BED), bulimia nervosa (BN) and anorexia nervosa (AN).

Pica involves compulsive eating of non-food items such as glass, plaster, sand, etc. for a period longer than one month. However, situations connected with certain developmental stages (e.g., young children putting various thing into their mouths) and motivated by culture (e.g., religious rituals or folk medicine methods) shall be excluded while diagnosing pica. Pica carries a risk of poisoning, iron deficiency and severe body damage (Blinder et al., 2008).

Rumination syndrome consists of passive and repeatable regurgitation of food from the stomach into the mouth following a meal which is then re-chewed and re-swallowed. The taste of regurgitated food is recognizable for patients and usually carries positive associations. Episodes most frequently last 1-2 hours or until the chime becomes sour and unpleasant-tasting. Rumination does not involve symptoms typical for vomiting: nausea, gag reflex, heartburn or stomach aches (Papadopoulos et al., 2007). The newest version of Diagnostic and Statistical Manual of Mental Disorders (i.e., DSM-V) does not indicate the age criterion for pica and rumination and both of them are currently diagnosed in patients of all ages.

Other eating disorders listed in DSM-V are far more frequent in general population than the two mentioned above. Binge eating disorder was introduced as a separate diagnosis quite recently, in DSM-V. In DSM-IV it was classified as eating disorder not otherwise specified (EDNOS). Introduction of binge eating disorder as a separate disease entity aimed at distinguishing it from overeating and emphasizing the acute nature of this disorder and its serious physical and mental consequences. BED is characterized by: repeatable episodes of voracity (eating considerably bigger amount of food than it is normal to eat in a given period of time by an average person), loss of control over quantity and quality of ingested food and the way of eating, emotionally triggered eating (e.g., because of anger, anxiety, depression, boredom) and a feeling of significant discomfort due to binge episodes (Cooper, Fairburn, 2003). BED occurs in 2.8 − 6.6% of general population and in 25% of obese people (Grucza et al., 2007, Hudson et al., 2007).

Bulimia nervosa consists of recurrent binge eating fits followed by compensatory behaviors (such as self-induced vomiting, the use of laxatives, etc.) aimed at preventing body weight increase. Binge eating fits are accompanied by the feeling of the loss of control and constant and exaggerated concern about body weight and measurements (Hay, Claudino, 2010). BN occurs in 0.1 – 9.4% of general population, in 2% of obese and in 16 – 52% of post-bariatric surgery patients (Fitzgibbon, Blackman, 2000; Makino et al., 2004). In DSM-V the diagnostic criterion of frequency of binge eating fits has been lowered both in case of BED and BN and established at the level of 1 fit per week for more than three months.

Anorexia nervosa manifests itself in distorted perception of patient's own body weight and body shape, obsessive fear of gaining weight in spite of remaining underweight and progressive self imposed restrictions over the amounts of food intake aimed at weight loss. DSM-V criteria for diagnosing AN no longer include the requirement of "refusal to maintain body weight at least at a level minimal for given age and height" since it can be difficult to assess. Instead a new criterion involving calorie-reducing behaviors was introduced. Moreover, the DSM-IV criterion requiring amenorrhea was deleted as it cannot be applied to males, pre-menarchal females, females taking oral contraceptives and post-menopausal females. AN occurs in 0.1 – 4.2% of general population (Treasure et al., 2003, Nogal et al., 2008).

It has been estimated that 90 – 95% of patients suffering from feeding and eating disorders (FED) are female (Kjelsås et al., 2004; Button et al., 2008). The following factors may contribute to such extensive domination of females among FED patients;

- biological factors (substantial increase in fatty tissue and changes of body shape at puberty may induce ambivalent emotions and the desire to return to child's silhouette);
- psychological (focusing on interpersonal relations and emotions is connected with strong need for being accepted in which the appearance plays a crucial role);
- socio-cultural (western patterns of beauty and appeal promote slim figure and are in conflict with consumerist lifestyle).

Because of restricted food intake or overeating FED can cause severe somatic health problems which may even lead to death (Nicholls, Grindrod, 2008; Czerwionka-Szaflarska et al., 2010; Florkowski et al., 2010). Mortality rate for AN fluctuates around 4 – 20% and is considered to be the highest among all mental disorders. About 50% of deaths in AN patients are due to electrolyte imbalance, others are a result of suicide (Dobrzyńska Rymaszewska, 2006; Papadopoulos et al., 2009). The risk of death in AN may increase due to the following factors: long-term suffering from AN, psychoactive drug abuse, low body mass and low psychosocial functioning (Franco et al., 2013).

Apart from causing physical damage, FED also impair patients' mental health and their social relations. The impairment manifests itself, inter alia, in the form of emotional disorders (e.g., anxiety, depression, obsessive-compulsive behavior, etc.), personality disorders, distorted body image, addictions, somatization and auto aggression. General quality of life also declines. Patients feel that eating or dieting gains control over their lives, they feel lonely and have low self-esteem. Patients' interpersonal relations become disturbed: patients manifest oversensitivity, perplexity, emotional instability, tendency to avoid social situations and interactions, especially when they are connected with eating (Reichborn-Kjennerud et al., 2004; Wilczek-Rużyczka, 2010). FED also correlate to disorders of sexual nature. Sex lives of people suffering from FED are of lower quality comparing to healthy people. Negative body image and the lack of control over eating cause decreased interest in other sex, lower sex drive, avoiding sexual contacts or the lack of arousal during sexual contacts (Sarol- Kulka, Kulka 2005; Castellini et al., 2010). Lower sex drive is particularly observed in females suffering from AN (Pinheiro et al., 2010).

The etiology of FED is a complex matter. Psychological factors (e.g., depression, emotional instability, low self-esteem and self-imposed high expectations, dissatisfaction with one's own body, the experience of appearance-related stigma or stress, etc.) are considered to play an important part in the development of FED. However, one shall not overlook genetic factors which are partially connected with psychological factors as they may affect personality (e.g., perfectionism, obsessiveness). The inheritance level of AN is estimated at 60%, whereas in case of BN it fluctuates around 30 – 40%. When it comes to biological point of view, dysfunctions of serotoninergic system seem to be relevant (Rybakowski, 2012).

Humans live in social environment which affects them incessantly. Literature on the subject of FED underlines the importance of family and its dysfunctionality in the development of FED, including such factors as: mood disorders and addictions of the parents, early separation from the parents, sexual abuse, unclear social roles, parents' negative beliefs about femininity and sexuality, excessive control or chaotic relations between parents and children (Striegel-Moore, 2007; Pilecki 2009). The reasons of the increasing incidence of FED are also to be seek in cultural influences, especially the ones connected with femininity. The ideal of slim figure currently prevalent in the western culture is often associated with strong will, success, perfectionism and control over one's life. Women are constantly under pressure over their appearance which should fit the prevalent ideal of feminine beauty. The ideal is based on the following criteria: age (forever young), type of beauty (classic, well-proportioned, womanly curved), height (long legs) and body weight (slim). The majority of women are incapable of meeting these expectations, if only because of their genetic predisposition. This, however, does not release them from feeling guilty and from constant pursuit of perfection. However, there might be differences in that matter among various races and nationalities. Amongst women most exposed to cultural influences we may list: white, oversensitive, dissatisfied with their bodies, with low self-esteem, prone to comparing themselves to other women, suffering from personality disorders and FED and teenagers (especially older teens, plump and having bulimic tendencies) (Durkin, 1999). It seems that cultural mechanisms may be far more influential in the development of bulimic disorders than in the development of AN (Pilecki et al., 2012).

Easily accessible media have an impact on female behaviors connected with eating and dieting for example by means of promoting the idea of dieting and slim body as a model of attractiveness, advertising high-calorie food and (almost at the same time) various drugs aiding weight loss, advertising size 0, presenting almost exclusively slim and beautiful women, reporting on the lives of celebrities who have spectacularly gained or lost weight, providing websites and message boards thanks to which the users motivate each other to lose weight and implement restrictive eating behaviors (Cuber, Grygiel, 2007).

We may name two social movements amongst the destructive influences of the internet, namely *thinspiration* (inspirations to become/maintain thin) and *pro-ana* (promotion of anorexia). The research on the number of Google search hits for the phrase "pro-ana blog" over the period of the years 2006 – 2010 has shown more than sixty-fold increase (Stochel, Janas-Kozik, 2010; Mantella, 2013). Virtual pro-ana communities support ego syntonic ideology presenting AN as a lifestyle and identity. Members of such groups support each other in preservation and deepening of malnutrition. Pro-ana internet diaries (blogs) users post pictures being the evidence of weight loss as well as meticulous descriptions of daily food intake (including the number of calories) which are then commented (either positively or negatively) and evaluated by other users (Talarczyk, Nitsch, 2010). The aim of the pro-ana community is to motivate its members to lose weight and share the ideas how to deceive family members for example by hiding food, distracting their attention when it comes to the appearance and weight of AN patient, cheating during weighing on the scales, etc. (Harshbarger et al., 2008). Pro-ana is considered dangerous as it promotes alarming behavior leading to self-starvation. On one hand, it offers support and the sense of belonging to a group, but on the other it may delay or impede the recovery or even preclude the patient from it (Stochel, Janas-Kozik, 2010).

The intermediary character of internet facilitates the communication of shy people. The relationships established via World Wide Web often are very deep and long lasting. Users interested in the matter may share the information about FED, contact each other via theme websites and message boards, send each other various articles, photographs or various diagnostic tests, but also addresses of Psychological Counseling Centers (Tukaj, 2005). Internet users often browse the web in search of methods for improving their health and wellbeing. German website providing information and counseling on FED called „Beratungs- und Informationsserver Essstörungen" has shown that there is a high demand for FED-related help among the internet users. Help was seek mostly by patients suffering from bulimia; other FED patients constituted only a small percentage of help seekers (BIE, 2013). The scope of the information seek by the internet users depends not only on the type of FED they represent but also (or even especially) on their age. In Poland people aged 16 – 24 constitute as many as 87% of the internet users (Polski internet, 2013).

For many people modern media such as the internet provide not only a source of information but also a platform for interpersonal relations. Internet users compare themselves with others, compete with one another, share their problems and successes and often emotionally support each other. Theme websites attract people with similar interests and preferences who by means of them wish to fulfill certain needs. The aim of the research was to estimate and evaluate the emotional state, the presence and the level of depression in the users of Polish websites on eating disorders and their attitude towards their own sexuality. These goals were planned to be achieved by the means of the analysis of the relationships between the researched variables.

MATERIAL AND METHOD

Participants

The research encompassed 200 females visiting Polish FED-themed websites or message boards and involved the use of retrospective questionnaires.

Method

Four tools were used in the course of the research: an original survey form, Emotional State Questionnaire (ESQ), Beck Depression Inventory (BDI) and Multidimensional Sexuality Self-Concept Questionnaire (MSSCQ).

An **original survey form** was designed specifically for the sake of this research. It included two sections: demographics/particulars (i.e., specification of age, body mass, height, interpersonal status, place of residence) and a set of 16 questions concerning: the frequency of visiting websites on FED, participants' beliefs about their own bodies, eating habits, dieting and subjective appraisal of their bodies. The participants were asked to answer the questions (in *demographic/particulars* section) or to decide to which extent the statements presented in the questionnaire apply to them (the other section). In order to enable the participants to identify with the presented statements colloquial vocabulary was used (e.g., "weight" instead of "body mass" or "fat" instead of "obese").

Emotional State Questionnaire (ESQ) was designed by I. Heszen-Niejodek and consists of the list of 15 emotions (i.e., optimism, doubt, fear, worry, hope, helplessness, joy, content, relief, excitement, anger, disappointment, satisfaction, eager and depression) concerning recent mood of the participant. Each emotion is followed by a set of numbers from 1 to 7. The participant is supposed to choose the number which applies to the level of his/her recent experiencing of that particular emotion. Number 1 stands for the lack of experiencing, 4 denotes mild intensity and 7 indicates the most intensive emotional experience. Certain questions form the following diagnostic categories: threat (fear of injury or damage), harm/loss (the feeling of damage), challenge (hope for profits), benefit (the feeling of profit). The results in particular categories are achieved by summing up certain items.

Beck Depression Inventory (BDI) consists of 21 multiple choice questions concerning respondents' recent mood. Each questions is followed by 4 choices of descriptive answers. Each answer has a certain number of points (from 0 to 3) assigned to it. The result is achieved by summing up the points assigned to the answers chosen by the respondent. The scale allows interpretation of the results and is based on the following criteria: 0–9 points indicate minimal depression, 10–18 indicate mild depression, 19–29 indicate moderate depression and 30–63: indicate severe depression.

Multidimensional Sexuality Self-Concept Questionnaire (MSSCQ) was designed by E. Snell and consists of 30 statements concerning various aspects of respondents' sex lives. The respondents are asked to mark the statements according to what extent they apply to them by using the following scale: 1 = not at all characteristic of me; 2 = slightly characteristic of me; 3 = somewhat characteristic of me; 4 = moderately characteristic of me; 5 = very characteristic of me. The statements form the following diagnostic categories: internal sexual control (defined as the belief that the sexual aspects of one's life are determined by one's own personal control), sexual motivation (defined as the motivation and desire to be involved in a sexual relationship), power-other sexual control (defined as the belief that the sexual aspects of one's life are controlled by others who are more powerful and influential than oneself), fear of sex (defined as a fear of engaging in sexual relations with another individual), sexual anxiety (defined as the tendency to feel tension, discomfort, and anxiety about the sexual aspects of one's life) and sexual satisfaction (defined as the tendency to be highly satisfied with the sexual aspects of one's life). The results in particular categories are achieved by summing up certain items.

Research Structure

Data gathering was conducted online. 14 Polish websites connected with the topic of FED (www.forum.zaburzeniaodzywiania.info, www.cpp.info.pl/forum, www.forum.narkotyki.pl, www.charaktery.eu, www.mam-efke.pl, www.zaburzenia.pl, www.forum.abczdrowie.pl, www.wizaż.pl, www.Polki.pl, www.gazeta.pl, www.forum.glodne.pl, www.psychocafe.pl, www.motylki.aaf.pl, www.nerwica.com) were featuring a link to a website created for the sake of this research in their sections devoted to eating disorders, anorexia, bulimia, binge eating, etc. The links were active for one month. The participation was voluntary and anonymous. The participants interested in the results of the research received e-mail addresses allowing them to contacts the authors.

Statistical Analysis

The analysis included all data gathered by means of an original survey form, ESQ, BDI and MSSCQ. Data analysis was conducted with the use of STATISTICA software package (STATISTICA 10 Copyright © StatSoft, 2011). In all forms and at all stages stages of the statistical analysis $\alpha = 0.05$ was chosen as the significance level. The probability distribution was measured by means of the Kolmogorov–Smirnov test. Due to the fact that the majority of distributions did not fit the Gaussian model, the authors decided to use nonparametric tests: Pearson's chi-squared test, Kruskal-Wallis one-way analysis of variance and Spearman's rank correlation coefficient.

The research was conducted in accordance with ethical and organizational guidelines of conducting scientific research at Medical University of Silesia.

RESULTS

The questionnaires were filled in by 230 respondents. However, only 200 were qualified as the participants in the research, as the rest of the respondents did not fill in the questionnaires completely or correctly which made the analysis impossible.

Participants' Profiles

The highest number of participants belonged to the age group between 16 and 25 (66%). The youngest participants were between 10 and 15 years old (21%). The majority of participants lived in a city (79%) and were single (65%). More details can be found in Table I.

As the group of the participants consisted of both adults and youth, BMI was interpreted only for participants over 16 in accordance with the World Health Organization classification for adults (WHO, 2004). The results were as follows: The majority's body mass was within the normal range (52%), 39% of respondents were underweight and 8.5% were overweight or obese.

Table I. Participants' profiles (QUALITATIVE data)

Variable		Number	Percentage
Age [category]	<10	0	0.00%
	10-15	41	21.00%
	16-20	71	36.00%
	21-25	60	30.00%
	26-30	16	8.00%
	>30	12	6.00%
	n/d	0	0.00%
Place of residence	Countryside	42	21.00%
	Town < 100 000 of residents	48	24.00%
	City > 100 000 of residents	110	55.00%
	n/d	0	0.00%
Interpersonal status	Single	129	65.00%
	In a relationship	71	36.00%
	n/d	0	0.00%

The table below presents the data on the height, body mass and BMI of the participants.

Table II. Participants' profiles (quantitative data)

Variable	N	Mean	Median	Min	Max	Standard deviation
Height [cm]	200	166.91	167	150	180	5.56
Body weight [kg]	200	55.91	54	33	160	14.61
BMI [kg/m^2]	200	20.02	19	13.55	55.36	4.76

Original Survey Form Data Analysis

The majority of the participants stated that they do not like their bodies (78.5%) and cannot control their body mass (52.5%). At the same time the majority of the participants are afraid of being/becoming obese (78%), treat controlling their weight as a meaning of their lives (51%), make their mood conditional of their body mass (72.5%), feel guilty after having too much to eat (72.5%), often think about food (76.5%), have the tendency to comfort-eating (51%) and because of their body mass wish they would not wake up one day (51%). A vast majority of the participants also believe that men prefer slim women (82.5%) (cf. Table III).

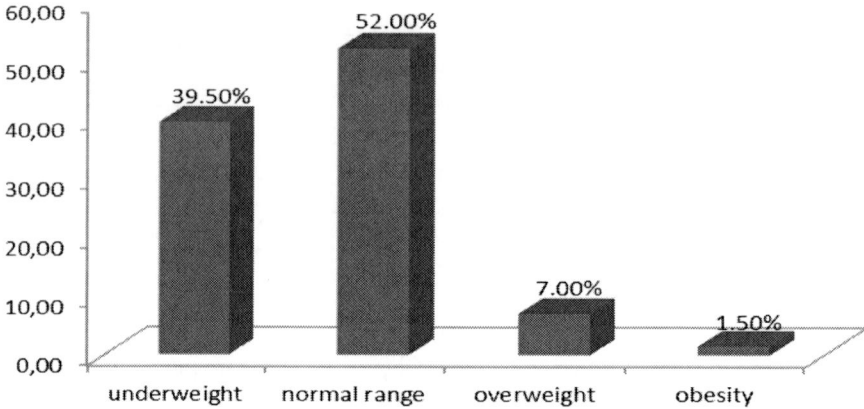

Figure I. Body mass of the participants aged >16.

Table III. Beliefs about participants' own bodies and eating habits

statement	definitely not/ rather not	I don't know	definitely yes/ rather yes
	%	%	%
I like my body	78.50	9.00	12.50
I feel I'm in control over my weight	52.50	11.00	36.50
I am afraid of gaining weight and being fat	11.50	1.50	87.00
Controlling my weight makes my life meaningful	28.50	20.50	51.00
My mood depends on my body weight	16.00	11.50	72.50
I feel guilty and I deserve to be punished after having eaten too much	16.00	8.50	75.50
I often think about eating	16.00	7.50	76.50
I eat in order to make myself feel better	36.50	12.50	51.00
Because of my weight I sometimes wish I wouldn't wake up	34.50	14.50	51.00
Men prefer slim women	3.00	14.50	82.50

The majority of participants declared they were currently on a diet (69.5%) and 47% of the participants admitted that they had been dieting for a year or more than one year. 73.5% of the participants consider themselves "too fat". Only 12.5% were satisfied with their figures and 5% believed they were too thin. The rest (9%) did not present any opinion about their figures. As many as 86% of the participants admitted they were thinking about their weight on a daily basis and 79% experienced low mood because of their weight.

The participants were also asked to determine how often they did visit FED connected websites and message boards. 32% of the participants answered "everyday", 23% "more than once a week, whereas 24.5% visit such websites less than once a week. The rest (20%) of the participants visited such sites only once or were not able to estimate how often they did. The participants most frequently declared searching for an effective weight loss method as the reason behind these visits (92%).

Emotional State Questionnaire (ESQ) Data Analysis

The table below (Table IV) shows raw scores achieved by the participants in the questionnaire.

Average scores in the categories of harm/loss and threat exceed the arithmetic mean of the possible scores in each category. Average scores in the categories of challenge and benefit, on the other hand, are below the arithmetic mean of the possible scores in each category.

Table IV. The results of the Emotional State Questionnaire (ESQ)

Variable		Mean	Med	Min	Max	St. dev.	Possible range
ESQ	harm/loss	16.08	18	3	21	4.77	3-21
	threat	22.41	24	6	28	5.78	4-28
	challenge	8.90	8	3	21	4.93	3-21
	benefit	11.06	10	4	25	5.40	4-28

N=200.

Beck Depression Inventory (BDI) Data Analysis

Raw scores achieved by the participants in the questionnaire are shown in Table V below.

Raw scores were recalculated into sten scores. The presence of depression varying in terms of intensity was diagnosed in 93% of the participants. 87% of the participants suffered from moderate or severe depression.

Multidimensional Sexuality Self-Concept Questionnaire (MSSCQ) Data Analysis

Raw scores of the questionnaire are presented in Table VI below.

Table V. The results of Beck Depression Inventory

Variable	Mean	Med	Min	Max	St. dev.	Possible range
BDI	30.37	31	1	57	12.18	0-63

N=200.

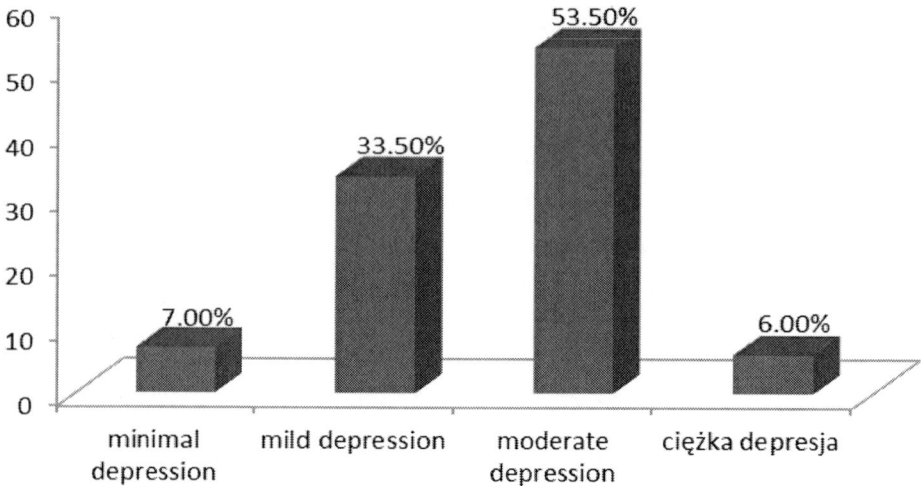

Figure II. The scale of depression of the participants according to BDI.

**Table VI. The results of the Multidimensional Sexuality
Self-Concept Questionnaire**

Variable		Mean	Med	Min	Max	St. dev.	Possible range
MSSCQ	internal sexual control	14.65	15	5	25	4.66	5-25
	sexual motivation	13.22	12	5	25	5.64	
	sexual anxiety	13.32	13	5	25	5.46	
	power-other sexual control	10.48	10	5	25	5.00	
	fear of sex	14.07	14	5	25	3.99	
	sexual satisfaction	10.89	10	5	25	5.14	

N=200.

Average scores in all categories are below the arithmetic mean of the possible scores in each category. The highest mean appeared in the category of internal sexual control, whereas the lowest means were observed in the categories of sexual satisfaction and power-other sexual control.

Statistical Analyses

The results demonstrated a statistically significant interdependence between the level of depression observed in the participants and their frequency of thinking about their body mass (p<0,001). The participants whose scores placed them in the category of suffering from severe depression were thinking about their body mass daily or more than once a week. The participants whose scores in BDI indicated lower levels of depression chose answers implying high frequency of thinking about their body mass much less frequently (Table VII).

What is more, the interdependence between the level of depression and the length of dieting period was observed. The participants whose BDI scores indicated depression (mild, moderate and severe) more often admitted they had been dieting for a year or more than a year than the participants whose BDI scores indicated minimal depression. The vast majority of the participants with scores indicating severe depression had been dieting for more than one year (Table VIII).

Table VII. The correlation between the frequency of thinking about one's body weight and the level of depression in the participants

			Beck Depression Inventory score				Altogether
			minimal depression	minimal depression	minimal depression	minimal depression	
The frequency of thinking about one's body weight	>1/week	Number	3	5	4	1	13
		%	23.10	38.50	30.80	7.70	100.00
	everyday	Number	4	58	99	11	172
		%	2.30	33.70	57.60	6.40	100.00
	<1/week	Number	4	2	1	0	7
		%	57.10	28.60	14.30	0.00	100.00
	not at all	Number	3	2	2	0	7
		%	42.90	28.60	28.60	0.00	100.00
	I don't know	Number	0	0	1	0	1
		%	0.00	0.00	100.00	0.00	100.00
Altogether		Number	14	67	107	12	200
		%	7,00	33.50	53.50	6.00	100,00

Test statistics

	Value	Df	Asymptotic 2-sided significance
Pearson's chi-square	54.79	12	**.000**
Likelihood ration	34.93	12	.000
Linear correlation test	4.58	1	.032
N of relevant observations	200		

Moreover, there was a statistically significant interdependence between the frequency of visiting websites on FED and low mood experienced by the participant because of their body mass. The highest number of participants who declared low mood problems visited FED-related websites daily (Table IX).

Table VIII. The correlation between the length of the dieting period and the level of depression in the participants

			Beck Depression Inventory score				Altogether
			minimal depression	mild depression	moderate depression	severe depression	
The length of the dieting period	None	Number	8	18	15	0	41
		%	19.50	43.90	36.60	0.00	100.00
	I don't know	Number	1	11	16	1	29
		%	3.44	37.91	55.23	3.42	100.00
	Less than a month	Number	3	6	9	1	19
		%	15.70	31.60	47.40	5.30	100.00
	More than a month	Number	2	6	9	0	17
		%	11.80	35.30	52.90	0.00	100.00
	About a year	Number	0	6	10	1	17
		%	0.00	35.30	58.80	5.90	100.00
	More than one year	Number	0	20	48	9	77
		%	0.00	26.00	62.30	11.70	100.00
Altogether		Number	14	67	107	12	200
		%	7.00	33.50	53.50	6.00	100.00

Test statistics

	Value	Df	Asymptotic 2-sided significance
Pearson's chi-square	33.29	15	**.004**
Likelihood ration	39.14	15	.001
Linear correlation test	23.02	1	.030
N of relevant observations	200		

Table IX. The correlation between the frequency of visiting websites on FED and low mood

			The frequency of visiting FED-related websites					Altogether
			Never	> 1/week	daily	< 1/week	Only once	
Low mood experienced because of one's body mass	No	Number	3	1	2	6	8	20
		%	15.00	5.00	10.00	30.00	40.00	100.00
	Yes	Number	15	41	59	34	9	158
		%	9.50	25.90	37.30	21.50	5.70	100.00
	I don't know	Number	5	5	3	9	0	22
		%	22.70	22.70	13.60	40.90	0.00	100.00
Altogether		Number	23	47	64	49	17	200
		%	11.50	23.50	32.00	24.50	8.50	100.00

Test statistics

	Value	Df	Asymptotic 2-sided significance
Pearson's chi-square	43.16	8	**.000**
Likelihood ration	36.21	8	.000
Linear correlation test	8.10	1	.004
N of relevant observations	200		

Apart from that, a statistically significant interdependence between the level of depression and the sense of harm/loss (R=0.60; p<0.05) and threat (R=0.59; p<0.05) has been proved. The more intense the symptoms of depression in participants, the bigger sense of harm/loss and threat they experience. The correlation between the level of depression and the sense of benefit (R=-0.51; p<0.05) and challenge (R=-0.30; p<0.05) has also been proved. The higher the level of depression in patients, the lower sense of benefit and challenge they experience.

There was also a statistically significant correlation between patients' sense of internal sexual control and their opinions on their figures. Participants who considered themselves "too fat" displayed lower internal sexual control than the participants who believe they were too thin or had a normal figure or did not specify their opinion (Table X).

Table X. The correlation between internal sexual control and the participants' opinions about their figures

Ranks			
	Participants' opinions about their figures	**N**	**Average rank**
ISC Internal Sexual Control	Normal	25	128.76
	Too fat	147	96.82
	Too thin	10	109.65
	I don't know	18	86.16
	Altogether	200	

Test statistics

	ISC Internal Sexual Control
Chi-square	9.57
df	3
Asymptotic 2-sided significance	**0.02**

No statistically significant relationship between BMI and the sense of threat or harm/loss has been proved as well as no statistically significant relationship between dieting and: the fear of sex, sexual anxiety, sexual motivation and the sense of benefit and challenge.

DISCUSSION

Internet has become and still becomes a more and more available medium, especially when it comes to young people. Taking FED into account, the internet provides an excellent source of knowledge for people suffering from FED or suspecting they might be suffering from FED. The world wide web allows also to share personal stories with others in full anonymity, and therefore, often encourages honesty and openness. It often happens so, that in case of people suffering from FED visiting FED-related websites the co-users are the only people aware of patients' problems and having insight into their recovery and struggle. The conducted research made an attempt at describing female users of Polish websites on eating disorders both in terms of socio-demographic factors and psychological factors. The research evaluated psychological wellbeing of the participants, their attitude towards their sexuality and the relationship between visiting FED-related websites and psycho-social functioning.

The BMI of the majority of the participants over 16 was normal, however, at the same time more than 75% of the participants considered themselves "too fat", displayed dissatisfaction with their bodies and admitted they are on slimming diet to reduce their weight. It may imply overly critical approach to their bodies and overestimating the size of their bodies. Distorted perception of one's own body is quite common, however the specificity of that distortion is sex-dependent. In general, women have a more negative perception of their bodies and opinion on them than men. Women are usually dissatisfied with their lower body parts and the higher their body mass, the more critical there are about their bodies (Kaschak, 2001; Zarek, 2007).

Other sources show that age is also an important factor which has an impact on women and their perception of their own bodies. Older women usually display bigger awareness of their real body image. Whereas young women are more subject to the discrepancies in the perception of their bodies. They much more often experience the clash between the *real I* and the *ideal I* (Izydorczyk, Rybicka-Klimczyk, 2009). Mass media play an important role in that process. Research carried out in Poland has shown that magazines directed at women, promoting slim and attractive images of women and slimming diets differ in the level of impact they have on the readers depending on the age of the readers. Pre-teens entering puberty (ca. 12 years old) declared an improvement of their mood after reading magazines, whereas older girls (ca. 17 years old) experienced significant mood falls. Such tendency may stem from the higher level of criticism displayed by older girls and the bigger external pressure considering their looks. It has also been observed that the mood and overall self-esteem in girls decrease with age (Mandal, 2004).

What is alarming, however, is the fact that in the conducted research negative body perception was declared also by girls under 15. The mere fact that 10- and 11-year-olds visit FED-related websites is a sign that the age of incidence for FED is decreasing. Once again, we may assume that this phenomenon is culture- and media-dependent, as promoting slim beauty ideals enhances the criticism towards one's own body and the pursuit of unrealistic goals already in very young girls. Research conducted by Sands (2010) has shown that body shape, body mass, body size and body color are factors which make up to 40 – 50% of the sense of satisfaction with one's own body in females. Health and fitness scored lower. Women's focus on the appearance is also connected with the progressing process of sexualization of girls and women which takes place in mass culture. It involves promoting sexuality as the key value, obligation and virtue of females. It leads to objectification of female body and debasement of other values, as well as encourages various mental disorders and lowers the quality of life in women (APA, 2011).

Though the majority of participants declared persistent thinking about their body mass and the ways to reduce it, thinking about food was mentioned almost as often. The participants try to control their mood by means of food and at the same time feel guilty after eating, experience low mood because of their weight and are afraid of gaining weight. Such behavior is characteristic of FED and may imply that female users of FED-related websites indeed do suffer from FED. The research involving Polish youth as participants conducted by Malara et al., (2010) has shown that 70% of the participants did not eat regularly, 22% dieted and felt guilty after eating. A small percentage of the participants admitted to using self-provoked vomiting as a method preventing from putting on weight. Almost 60% of the participants believed underweight was more desirable than overweight. The following symptoms were diagnosed in the participants: sleep problems, hair fall, brittle nails, concentration and attention deficiencies. The results suggested presence of abnormal eating habits and the threat of FED in the participants.

The conducted research has shown that 80% of the participants suffer from low mood because of their current weight and more than 1/3 declared that "sometimes they wish they wouldn't wake up". For the participants dieting is not connected with the sense of benefit. They perceive dieting negatively and they do not derive satisfaction from it. Quite the contrary, the participants experience sense of harm/loss and threat. Musci et al., (2013) report that there is a significant correlation between suffering from FED and teenage suicides. The conducted research has shown that female users of FED-related websites display a tendency for the incidence of depression. The symptoms of depression, varying in terms of intensity, have been noted in 93% of the participants. Depression is yet another disorder which in many cases leads to suicide (attempts). The variety of symptoms it displays and the presence of the form of masked depression (MD) make it very hard to diagnose. Depression is characterized by low mood, agitated or lethargic behavior, anxiety, guilt, eating disorders, sleeping disorders, low libido, concentration problems, memory deficiency, etc. (Eisendrath et al., 2012).

In the conducted research a relationship between weight motivated low mood and the frequency of visiting FED-related websites has been observed. The more often the participants visit such websites, the lower mood they experience. This correlation may be two-sided which means that either low mood motivates visiting FED-related websites or the fact of visiting influences the mood. The significant number of participants visited such websites everyday, which may imply strong attachment to such form of sharing emotions or seeking information in case of patients diagnosed with FED or suspecting such diagnosis. It may be deduced that low mood is a stimulus so to speak to seek help online or to anonymously express one's feelings in the internet.

Multiple research point out the negative impact of the perception of one's body and of the FED on the sexuality. It has been proved that women suffering from FED display lower sexual activity with their partners and have a six time bigger chance of suffering from sexual disorders than healthy women. Moreover, in case of women suffering FED masturbation is more often the only form of sexual activity (Sarol- Kulka, Kulka, 2005; Mazzei et al., 2011). Only 1/3 of the participants in the conducted research were in relationship. The rest of the participants were single. The participants who considered their figure satisfying had a significantly higher level of internal sexual control than the participants who claimed they were "too fat" or did not present any opinion on their bodies. Internal sexual control shall be understood as the belief that the sexual aspects of one's life are determined by one's own personal control. Respondents of MSSCQ who achieve high scores in that category are more assertive when it comes to sex, have less doubts and experience more pleasure than the ones who score less. The participants displayed a low level of power-other control which means they believe that other people or fate do not have more impact on their sex lives than they themselves. It may be a result of dieting which gives a bigger sense of control over one's live and the ability to decide on one's own. However, the relationship between dieting and sexual motivation has not been proved. It may suggest that taking measures to improve physical attractiveness does not affect significantly the attitude towards one's own sexuality and a real or potential partner.

Internet as a source providing respondents for scientific research has both supporters and objectors. However, taking into account the facts that the number of people with internet access is continually growing and having a PC with internet access becomes a common thing it seems well grounded to use electronic form of data gathering. Its unquestioned advantages include providing full anonymity and the speed of the transfer of information. On the other hand, such method has its limitations such as the possibility of lowered representativeness of the sample. Because of the abundance of surveys and questionnaires generated by marketing and market research companies internet users tend to reject such forms without even taking a look at their contents. It may result in a narrow scope of respondents consisting of people particularly interested in the subject and therefore for example displaying a high intensity of a given disorder or having specific personality traits (e.g., neuroticism, extraversion, etc.). If the conducted research was to be expanded it would be advisable to include information concerning character traits of the respondents and their motivation to visit FED-related websites.

CONCLUSION

1. Female users of Polish websites on FED:
   - experience the sense of harm/loss and threat, do not accept their bodies and are preoccupied with thinking about their weight, about food and about dieting;
   - display the symptoms of depression varying in terms of their intensity;
   - are anxious about sex and sexual relationships and their sexual satisfaction is lowered, however, at the same time they have motivation for having sex and believe they can control their sex lives;
2. The preoccupation with body mass and dieting is connected with the escalation of the symptoms of depression and decrease in the sense of control over one's own sexuality. The depression resulting from the lack of acceptation of one's own body increases the frequency of visiting FED-related websites.

REFERENCES

American Psychiatric Association. (2013). *Diagnostic and statistical manual of mental disorders* (5th ed.). Arlington, VA: American Psychiatric Publishing.

APA Task Force on the Sexualization of Girls; http://www.apa.org/about/gr/pi/advocacy/2011/sexualization.aspx

Beratungs- und Informationsserver zu Essstoerungen (online). Dostępne: http://www.ab-server.de/. Pobrano 8.01.2013 r.

Blinder, B. J. & Salama, C. (2008). An update on Pica: prevelance, contributing causes, and treatment. *Psychiatric Times, 25*(6), 66-73.

Button, E., Aldridge, S. & Palmer, R. (2008). Males assessed by a specialized adult eating disorders service: Patterns over time and comparisons with females. *The International Journal of Eating Disorders, 41*(8), 758-61.

Castellini, G., Mannucci, E., Mazzei, C., Lo Sauro, C., Faravelli, C., Rotella, C. M., Maggi, M. & Ricca, V. (2010). Sexual function in obese women with and without binge eating disorder. *The Journal of Sexual Medicine, 7*(12), 3969-3978.

Cooper, Z. & Fairburn, C. G. (2003). Refining the definition of binge eating disorder and nonpurging bulimia nervosa. *The International Journal of Eating Disorders, 34* (Suppl), 89–95.

Cuber, T. & Grygiel, J. (2007). Wpływ Internetu na występowanie zjawiska anoreksji. *Pielęgniarstwo XXI w.*, 20-21(3-4), 65-70.

Czerwionka-Szaflarska, M., Jakubowska-Zając, B., Zielińska, I. & Maćkowska, P. (2010). Zaburzenia odżywiania o podłożu psychogennym u dzieci i młodzieży. *Klinika Pediatryczna, 18*(2), 255-258.

Dobrzyńska, E. & Rymaszewska, J. (2006). Jadłowstręt psychiczny- ciągłe wyzwanie dla współczesnej medycyny. *Psychiatria w Praktyce Ogólnolekarskiej, 6*(4), 165-170.

Durkin, S. (1999). *Relationship between female's body image and the mass media*. Melbourn: Body Image and Health Inc.

Eisendrath, S. J. & Lichtmacher, J. E. (2012). Psychiatric disorders. In: L.M. Tierney, M.A. Papadakis & S.J. McPhee (ed.). *Current Medical Diagnosis & Treatment*. New York, N.Y.: The McGraw-Hill Companies.

Fitzgibbon, M. & Blackman, L. (2000). Binge eating disorder and Bulimia nervosa: Differences in the Quality and Qantity of Binge Eating Episodes. *The International Journal of Eating Disorders, 27*, 238-243.

Florkowski, A., Kryszkowski, W., Bobińska, K. & Chojnacki, C. (2010). Gastroenterologiczne objawy i powikłania bulimii. *Gastroenterologia, 7*(6), 12-15.

Franko, D. L., Keshaviah, A., Eddy, K. T., Krishna, M., Davis, M. C., Keel, P. K. & Herzog, D. B. (2013). A longitudinal investigation of mortality in anorexia nervosa and bulimia nervosa. *The American Journal of Psychiatry, 170*(8), 917-925.

Grucza, R. A., Przybeck, T. R. & Cloninger, C. R. (2007). Prevalence and correlates of binge eating disorder in a community sample. *Comprehensive Psychiatry*, *48*(2), 124-131.

Harshbarger, J. L., Ashlers-Schmidt, C. R., Mayans, L., Mayans, D. & Hawkins, J. (2008). Pro-anorexia Web sites: What a clinical should know. *The International Journal of Eating Disorders*, *29*, 376-380.

Hay, P. J. & Claudino, A. M. (2010). Bulimia nervosa. *Clinical Evidence* (Online), 1009.

Hudson, J. I., Hiripi, E., Pope, H. G. & Kessler, R. C. (2007). The prevalence and correlates of eating disorders in the National Comorbidity Survey Replication. *Biological Psychiatry*, *61*, 348-358.

Izodorczyk, B. & Rybicka-Klimczyk, A. (2009). Środki masowego przekazu i ich rola w kształtowaniu wizerunku ciała u zróżnicowanych wiekiem życia kobiet polskich (analiza badań własnych). *Problemy Medycyny Rodzinnej*, *11*(3), 20-32.

Kashak, E. (2001). *Nowa psychologia kobiety. Podejście feministyczne*. Gdańsk: GWP.

Kjelsås, E., Bjørnstrøm, C. & Götestam, K. G. (2004). Prevalence of eating disorders in female and male adolescents (14-15 years). *Eating Behaviors*, *5*(1), 13-25.

Makino, M., Tsuboi, K. & Dennerstein, L. (2004). Prevalence of eating disorders: a comparison of Western and non-Western countries. *Medscape General Medicine*, *6*(3), 49.

Malara, B., Jośko, J., Kasperczyk, J. & Kamecka-Krupa, J. (2010). Rozpowszechnienie zaburzeń odżywiania wśród młodzieży w wybranych miastach województwa śląskiego. *Problemy Higieny i Epidemiologii*, *91*(3), 388-392.

Mandal, E. (2004). The influence of youth magasines on mood and self – image of Polish girls in early and late adolescence – The role of self – affirmation mechanisms in the integration of attractiveness, intellectual and interpersonal competence. *Polish Psychological Bulletin*, *35* (4), 217 – 224.

Mantella, D. G. *Pro-ana web-log uses and gratifications: towards understanding the pro-anorexia paradox* (online). Dostępne: http:// digitalarchive.gsu.edu/cgi/viewcontent.cgi?article=1023&context=commu nication_theses&seiedir=1&referer=http%3A%2F%2Fwww.google.pl%2 Fsearch%3Fq%3Dmantella%2BDG%2Bpro%2Bana%2Bparadox%26rlz %3D1C1SKPL_enPL446PL447%26oq%3Dmantella%2BDG%2Bpro%2 Bana%2B. Pobrane 8.01.2013 r.

Mazzei, C., Castellini, G., Benni, L., Godini, L., Lazzeretti, L., Pracucci, C., Talamba, G. A., Ricca, V. & Faravelli, C. (2011). Sexuality and eating disorders. *Rivista di Psichiatia*, *46*(2), 122-8.

Musci, R. J., Hart, S. R. & Ialongo, N. (2013). Internalizing Antecedents and Consequences of Binge Eating Behaviors in a Community-Based, Urban Sample of African American Females. *Prevention Science*; DOI 10.1007/s11121-013-0411-9

Nicholls, D. & Grindrod, C. (2008). Behavioural eating disorders. *Journal of Paediatrics and Child Health*, *2*(19), 60-66.

Nogal, P. & Lewiński, A. (2008). Anorexia Nervosa. *Polish Journal of Endocrinology*, *59*(2), 148–155.

Papadopoulos, F. C., Ekbom, A., Brandt, L. & Ekselius, L. (2009). Excess mortality, causes of death and prognostic factors in anorexia nervosa. *The British Journal of Psychiatry*, *194*(1), 10-7.

Papadopoulos, V. & Mimidis, K. (2007). The rumination syndrome in adults: A review of the pathophysiology, diagnosis and treatment. *Journal of Postgraduate Medicine*, *53*(3), 203–206.

Pilecki, M. W. (2009). Psychogenic determinants of bulimia nervosa. *Przegląd Lekarski*, *66*(1-2), 106-109.

Pilecki, M. W., Józefik, B. & Sałapa, K. (2012). The cultural context of eating disorders--own research. *Psychiatria Polska*, *46*(2), 189-200.

Pinheiro, A. P., Raney, T. J., Thornton, L. M., Fichter, M. M., Berrettini, W. H., Goldman, D., Halmi, K. A., Kaplan, A. S., Strober, M., Treasure, J., Woodside, D. B., Kaye, W. H. & Bulik, C. M. (2010). Sexual functioning in women with eating disorders. *The International Disorders*, *43*(2), 123-129.

Polski Internet 2008/2009 (online). Dostępne: http://pliki.gemius.pl/Raporty /2009/02_2009_Polski_internet_2008_2009.pdf. Pobrane 8.01. 2013 r.

Reichborn-Kjennerud, T., Bulik, C. M., Sullivan, P. F., Tambs, K. & Harris, J. R. (2004). Psychiatric and medical symptoms in binge eating in the absence of compensatory behaviors. *Obesity Research*, *12*, 1445-1454.

Rybakowski, F. (2012). Podstawy kliniczne. In: K. Jaracz, J. Rybakowski & K. Górna (ed.). *Pielęgniarstwo psychiatryczne*. Warszawa: PZWL, 295-306.

Sands, R. (2000). Reconceptualization of Body Image and Drive for Thinness. *The International Journal of Eating Disorders*, *28*(4), 397 – 407.

Sarol- Kulka, A. & Kulka, Z. (2005). Obraz własnego ciała a seksualność kobiet z zaburzeniami odżywiania się. *Postępy Psychiatrii i Neurologii*, *14*(2), 115-122.

Stochel, M. & Janas-Kozik, M. (2010). Przyjaciółka wirtualnej Any- zjawisko proanoreksji w sieci internetowej. *Psychiatria Polska*, *44* (5), 693-702.

Striegel-B., Taylor, C. B. & Daniels, S. R. (2007). Risk factors for binge-eating disorders: an exploratory study. *The International Journal of Eating Disorders*, *40*(6), 481-487.

Talarczyk, M. & Nitsch, K. (2010). Zaburzenia odżywiania się w portalach internetowych- opis i analiza zjawiska. *Psychoterapia*, *152* (1), 67-80.

Treasure, J., Claudino, A. M. & Zucker, N. (2010). Eating disorders. *Lancet*, *375*(9714), 583-593.

Tukaj, D. (2005). Anoreksja i bulimia w Internecie. *Lekarz*, *4*, 32.

WHO expert consultation. (2004). Appropriate body-mass index for Asian populations and its implications for policy and intervention strategies. *The Lancet*, *363*(9403), 157-163.

Wilczek-Rużyczka, E. (2010). Konsekwencje anoreksji w sferze psychicznej, somatycznej i funkcjonowaniu społecznym. In: D. Kurpas, L. Sochocka & A. Stewicko (ed.). *Dziecko i jego środowisko. Wyzwania pediatrii w XXI wieku- problemy zdrowotne dzieci w wieku szkolnym*. Wrocław: Wydawnictwo Continuo, 45-54.

Zarek, A. (2007). Porównanie subiektywnej oceny ciała mężczyzn i kobiet w wieku 19-25 lat. *Rocznik Pomorskiej Akademii Medycznej w Szczecinie*, *53*(3), 26-33.

In: Psychology of Habits   ISBN: 978-1-62948-959-9
Editor: Robin Mazzariello   © 2014 Nova Science Publishers, Inc.

Chapter 2

SLEEP, TELEVISION, TEXTING AND COMPUTER HABITS AND OVERWEIGHTNESS IN SCHOOLCHILDREN AND ADOLESCENTS

Pernilla Garmy[*1,2]
[1]Center for Primary Health Care Research, Lund University, Lund, Sweden
[2]Department of Health Science, Kristianstad University,
Kristianstad, Sweden

ABSTRACT

This chapter provides a synthesis of three earlier published studies (Garmy et al., 2012[a]; Garmy et al., 2012[b]; Garmy et al., 2013) (survey I) as well as previously unpublished results from a survey conducted in 2013 among students aged 16 (survey II).

Objective: The aim was to investigate the effects of sleep, television use and texting and computer habits on overweight, enjoyment of school and feelings of tiredness at school in school-age children and adolescents.

Methods: This cross-sectional study was conducted in Sweden on schoolchildren aged 6, 7, 10, 14 and 16. A questionnaire which had been satisfactorily tested for validity and reliability was distributed to the children (n=3011 in survey I; n=204 in survey II*)*.

Results: Children who slept less than the median length of time reported enjoying school to a lesser degree. Fewer hours of sleep were

* Corresponding address: Pernilla Garmy, Department of Health Sciences, Kristianstad University, SE-291 88 Kristianstad, Sweden. E-mail: Pernilla.garmy@hkr.se.

found to be associated with having a bedroom television, using the television or computer more than 2 hours a day, being tired at school, and having difficulties in sleeping and waking up. Overweight and obesity were found in 15.8% of the study population; obesity alone was found in 3.1%. Relationships between lifestyle factors and overweight were studied using multivariate logistic regression analysis. Having a bedroom television and using the television more than 2 hours per day were found to be associated with overweight, but using the computer more than 2 hours a day was not. About 61% of the students aged 16 reported checking Facebook or social media at least once a day, and 27% reported doing so more than 10 times a day. One fourth of the students aged 16 had a habit of sending or receiving text messages at night at least once a week. Texting at night and frequent checking of Facebook and social media sites were related to sleep problems.

Conclusions: Educating schoolchildren and their parents regarding matters of optimal sleep and how media habits affect sleep, overweight and learning is considered an important task.

BACKGROUND

Children's sleep problems need to be taken seriously. Longitudinal studies have shown that lack of sleep in children increases the risk of mental illness in adult age (Gregory et al., 2008). It is important for health and medical care professionals to have a finely-tuned instinct about this issue. Although we are aware of sleep's fundamental role in a child's physical and mental health, we also know that all children have periods when they sleep badly, and parents should not need to be concerned unnecessarily. In adults there is a connection between obesity and extremely short or long periods of sleep. This relationship is not as pronounced in children, but a newly published study by Spruyt et al., (2011) shows that children with obesity are at risk of developing irregular sleeping habits, are less likely to catch up on their sleep at weekends and have shorter periods of sleep. In combination, this will have adverse consequences on their metabolism. Lack of sleep affects the immune defence system, memory retention, learning capability, growth, insulin sensitivity and blood lipids, among other things. Sleep is an anabolic, restorative and building process. In children, insufficient sleep can lead to lapses in concentration, mood swings and impulse control problems during the day (Kryger et al., 2011).

In puberty, many students become "night people" who dislike getting up in the morning. Puberty entails both a huge hormonal readjustment and a period of accelerated growth. Night people accumulate a "sleep deficit" during the school week, as they stay up late but still have to get up early to go to school. It is common for night people to skip breakfast and to feel tired at school. On average, students who eat breakfast get higher grades (Adolphus et al., 2013). Even if this relationship may be influenced by other factors such as the family's socio-economic status, it is nevertheless a useful argument for improving children's breakfast habits. Many teenagers end up with a delayed circadian clock which can create problems with their school work. A delayed circadian clock does not automatically mean you have problems falling asleep or have other sleep problems; it means you have moved your sleep period out of sync with society at large. One example is Erik in the first grade of upper-secondary school. He plays computer games at night with friends in other parts of the world. As a result, he falls asleep in the early hours of the morning at around 4 or 5 a.m. Then he sleeps for 7 hours and wakes up refreshed at around 11 a.m. or 12 noon. Erik therefore misses a large part of the school day and, as a result, risks getting poor grades.

In a controlled study (Wahlstrom 2010) in Minnesota, US, students in one part of the school district were given one hour of extra sleep in the morning, while students in the other part observed the regular times. The children who were allowed to 'sleep in' made better grades, had less irregular sleep habits, felt less tired at school, felt better and were less prone to depression and antisocial behaviour. Furthermore, the teachers said that their own working conditions improved: there was more time for planning and classes were more orderly. Parents too reported positive changes with the extra sleep. The students ate breakfast more frequently. But the question is this: By shifting the start of the school day by one hour, do we actually affect the students' tendencies to stay up late at nights? It is possible that the successful results in these studies indicate that youngsters simply got more sleep while the study was in progress. The real question is whether they continued to go to bed at reasonable times when the study was finished, or whether they delayed the 'clock' even more.

AIM

The aim was to investigate how sleep, television use and texting and computer habits affected overweight, enjoyment and feelings of tiredness at school in school-age children and adolescents.

METHODS

Study Setting and Participants

Survey I was conducted in 2008-2009 in association with school health services in southern Sweden. In accordance with national policy, all students enrolled in the primary class (6 years) and in grades 1, 4, 8, and 10 (ages 7, 10, 14, and 16 years, respectively) are offered an individual health visit with the school nurse. In October 2013, survey II was conducted in grade 10 (16 years) in one school.

Instruments

Students wearing light clothing were weighed to the nearest 0.1 kg on a standard digital scale. Their height without shoes was measured to the nearest 0.1 cm using a manual height board. BMI (body mass index) was calculated and assessed using the international age- and gender-specific BMI cut-off points for children and adolescents to define overweight and obesity (Cole et al., 2000). Those with BMI of at least 25 kg/m^2 were classified as overweight, and those with a BMI corresponding to at least 30 kg/m^2 as obese.

To record sleep, television and computer habits of school-age children, a questionnaire was developed and its validity and reliability tested (Garmy et al., 2012[a]). The questionnaire's validity was evaluated on three aspects: face validity, content validity and construct validity. To assess the stability of the questionnaire, it was distributed to 138 respondents once, and again after two weeks. The questionnaire was found to be valid and reliable (ibid). The eleven questions on the questionnaire recorded whether the child had a television set in the bedroom (yes/no), how many hours/minutes the child spent watching television per day, the same for computer use, how much the child enjoyed school (very much, fairly well, not much at all), how often the child felt tired at school (never, seldom, often, every day), how often the child had difficulty getting up in the morning (never, seldom, often, every morning), and how many hours/minutes the child slept per night. Gender and year of birth were also recorded. In survey II, two questions regarding texting at night (never, approximately 3–10 times a year, at least once a month, at least once a week) and use of social media such as Facebook (never, every week, every day, > 10 times a day) were added.

Ethical issues

Informed consent was obtained, and the students and their parents were informed that participation was voluntary. The study was approved by the Advisory Committee on Research Ethics in Health Education (VEN 34-09) at Lund University.

Data Collection

Survey I

Height and weight measurements were collected by school nurses (n=32) during students' regular health visit at school health services, at which the nurses also distributed the questionnaire. All students filled out their own questionnaires, except the youngest students (ages 6 and 7), whose parents filled out the questionnaires. The questionnaire was distributed to 3011 out of a total population of 4692 students (64.9%). Lack of time on the part of school nurses resulted in the questionnaire not being distributed to all students. In primary and grade 1 classes, 569 students participated, in addition to 635 from grade 4, 782 from grade 8 and 1025 from grade 10. Girls comprised 49.7% of the cohort. Only 1.3% of students given the questionnaire declined to participate. Weight and height measurements were recorded for 2891 (95.9%) participating students.

Survey II

All students in grade 10 (n=260) at a science and technology high school were asked to answer the questionnaire. The response rate was 78.5% (n=204). Girls comprised 42% of the cohort.

Data Analysis

Children were classified as overweight or obese if their BMI values exceeded the international age- and gender-specific BMI cut-off points developed by Cole et al., (2000). All other independent variables, such as tiredness at school, difficulty in falling asleep, and difficulty in waking up, were treated as dichotomous with scores of 0 (seldom or never) and 1 (often or every day). For the question regarding enjoyment of school, answers were scored as 0 (very much) or 1 (moderate or no enjoyment). Daily television and computer use were dichotomised at 2 hours, in line with recommendations of the American Academy of Pediatrics (2001). Sleep length was dichotomous with scores of 0 (sleeping at least the median length of time) or 1 (sleeping less than the median). Relationships between factors associated with being overweight or obese were analysed using multiple logistic regression (enter) (Norman and Streiner 2008). Quality of the regression model was measured using the Hosmer and Lemeshow goodness-of-fit test and the Nagelkerke R^2 test. P-values of ≤ 0.05 were considered statistically significant. All statistical analyses were performed using SPSS (version 17.0).

Synthesis of the Results from Survey I

Overweight

Overweight and obesity were found in 16.7% of the study population (Garmy et al., 2013), with age groups broken down as follows: ages 6–7, 17.6%; age 10, 18.4%; age 14, 16.9%; age 16, 15.1%. Obesity alone was found in 2.8–3.8% of the population, depending on age group, with an average of 3.2%. Overweight was associated with having a bedroom television (OR 1.26) and television use exceeding 2 hours per day (OR 1.55) but not with computer use exceeding 2 hours per day, sleep duration less than the median, low enjoyment of school, tiredness at school or difficulties in sleeping and /or waking up (ibid).

Sleep

Each consecutive age group was found to have a later median bedtime: 8:00 PM for ages 6–7, 9:00 PM for age 10, 10:30 PM for age 14, and 11:00 PM for age 16 (Garmy et al., 2012[b]). The children took 0.5–1 hour to get ready for bed. The median length of sleep per night decreased for each consecutive group: 10 hours for ages 6–7, 9.5 hours for age 10, 8 hours for age 14, and 7.5 hours for age 16. All ages slept an average of 10 hours a night on weekends. The youngest group generally showed stable sleep patterns every night, but the three older age groups showed increased sleep on weekends compared with weekdays: 0.5 hours more for age 10, 2 hours more for age 14, and 2.5 hours more for age 16 (Table 1).

Table 1. Length of sleep in schoolchildren, weeknights (n=3011), (Garmy et al., 2012[b])

Age	Sleep length	Bedtime
6–7	10 hours	20:00
10	9.5 hours	21:00
14	8 hours	22:30
16	7.5 hours	23:00

Falling asleep with difficulty was reported in fewer than 10% children in the youngest group (ages 6–7) but nearly 20% children in the older age groups. Often being tired at school was reported by few (2.5%) children aged 6–7, nearly 20% of children aged 10 and over 40% of adolescents. Waking up with difficulty was experienced by close to 19% of children aged 6–7, 39% of children aged 10, and the majority of the adolescents. Although most of the children and adolescents stated that they enjoyed school very much, adolescents aged 14 reported that they enjoyed school the least. Less than 60% of this group enjoyed school very much, compared with more than 70% of all the other age categories.

The participants in each age group were categorised according to sleep duration: short (those sleeping less than the median for their grade) and long (those sleeping the median or longer). Children with short sleep duration reported enjoying school to a significant lesser extent. Multiple logistic regression analysis revealed significant correlations between short sleep duration and being tired at school, falling asleep and waking up with difficulty, having a television in the bedroom, and television or computer use exceeding 2 hours.

Television and Computer Habits

Having a television in the bedroom was more prevalent among consecutively older age groups: 21% of children aged 6–7, 31% of children aged 10, 49% of children aged 14 and 58% of children aged 16. The youngest two age groups (ages 6–7 and age 10) reported 1 hour of television use per day, whereas the oldest two groups (age 14 and 16) reported 1.5 hours of daily television use. Television use exceeding 2 hours per day was found in 21% of children aged 6–7, 30% of children aged 10, 44% of children aged 14, and 41% of children aged 16. Computer use started at 0.5 hours per day among children aged 6–7 and rose to 1 hour for age 10 and 2 hours for ages 14 and 16. Computer use exceeding 2 hours per day was found in only 2% of children aged 6–7 but in 20% of children aged 10, 53% of children aged 14 and 62% of children aged 16 (Garmy et al., 2012[b]).

RESULTS FROM SURVEY II

In a survey of 204 students in grade 10 (aged 16), 61% reported checking Facebook or other social media sites at least once a day. About 27% reported checking it more than 10 times a day. Although 38% reported that they never sent or received text messages on their cell phone at night, 28% did so at least once a week (see Table 2). Length of sleep, television, computer, social media and texting habits, feelings of being tired, feeling of enjoying school, and difficulties in falling asleep and in waking up are presented in Table 3. Median length of sleep on weeknights was 8 hours, compared with 10 hours on weekends. About 24% of the students spent two hours or more each day watching television, but 66% spent two hours or more at the computer each day (not school-related). About 17% reported often having difficulties falling asleep, and 49% were often tired in school.

Table 2. Prevalence of checking Facebook or social media and texting at night in grade 10 (students aged 16, n=204)

I check Facebook or social media	18 (9%) Never	5 (2%) Every week	155 (34%) Every day	55 (27%) > 10 times a day	11 (5%) other
I send or receive text messages on my cell phone at night	79 (38%) Never	30 (15%) About 3–10 times a year	23 (11%) At least once a month	57 (28%) At least once a week	15 (7%) other

Those sending or receiving text messages at night at least once a week reported having shorter sleep on weeknights, being tired in school more frequently, enjoying school to a lesser extent, having greater difficulties both sleeping and waking up, later bedtimes (both on weekdays and weekends), waking up later on weekends, and more frequently checking Facebook or other social media sites (Table 4). In the multiple logistic regression analysis carried out, texting at night at least once a week was found to be significantly related to checking Facebook or social media more than 10 times a day, and late bedtime on weekends (Table 5).

Those checking Facebook or other social media sites more than 10 times a day reported being tired in school more frequently, having more difficulties in falling asleep, having shorter sleep, and going to bed later on weeknights (Table 6).

Table 3. Length of sleep in school grade 10 (students aged 16), and their television, computer, social media and texting habits, feelings of being tired, feeling of enjoying school, and difficulties in falling asleep and in waking up (n=204)

Median length of sleep on weeknights (IQR)	8 h (1 h)
Median length of sleep on weekends (IQR)	10 h (2 h)
Median time spent getting ready for bed (IQR)	9:15 p.m. (1 h 45 m)
Median bedtime weekdays (IQR)	10:30 p.m. (1 h)
Median waking time weekdays (IQR)	6:30 a.m. (1 h)
Median bedtime weekends (IQR)	12:00 p.m. (2½ h)
Median waking time weekends (IQR)	10:00 a.m. (2 h)
Median time in hours watching TV (IQR)	1h (1½ h)
Median time at the computer (IQR)	2½ h (3 h)
Two hours or more watching TV each day	47 (24%)
Two hours or more at the computer each day	131 (66%)
Often has difficulties falling asleep	35 (17%)
Enjoys school very much	130 (65%)
Often tired in school	98 (49%)
Often has difficulties waking up	123 (61%)

DISCUSSION

The factors found to be associated with less sleep were having a television in the bedroom, television or computer use in excess of 2 hours per day, and having difficulty going to sleep and waking up. Children who slept less than their peers reported significantly less enjoyment of school (Garmy et al., 2012[b]). Overweight was associated with having a bedroom television and television use of more than 2 hours per day (Garmy et al., 2013). Overall prevalence of overweight and obesity, which were found in about 18% of the children aged 6–10, is consistent with other studies (Sjöberg et al., 2011; Sjöberg et al., 2008; Sundblom et al., 2008; Lager et al., 2009).

Table 4. Sending or receiving text messages at night at least once a week (n=204)

	Texting at night (at least once a week) n=57 (28%)	Not texting at night (less than once a week) n=147 (72%)	p value[a]
Tired in school	33 (61%)	61 (41%)	0.028*
Difficulties falling asleep	18 (33%)	20 (14%)	0.010*
Difficulties waking up	41 (76%)	75 (51%)	0.019*
Enjoying school very much	30 (55%)	93 (63%)	0.033*
Short sleep (less than 8 h)	32 (56%)	37 (25%)	0.001*
Late bedtime on weeknights (after 10:30 p.m.)	27 (47%)	41 (28%)	0.034*
Waking up late on weekends (after 10 a.m.)	30 (55%)	48 (33%)	0.031*
Late bedtime on weekends (after 12 a.m.)	37 (65%)	50 (34%)	0.001*
Checking Facebook or social media >10 times a day	27 (47%)	23 (16%)	<0.001*
Being female	27 (47%)	42 (29%)	0.019*

[a] Chi-square test.

Children aged 6 and 7 slept for a median of 10 hours on weeknights. This corresponds with the sleep recommendation for children aged 6–12, which is 10–11 hours. However, children aged 10 only slept a median of 9.5 hours, which is less than the recommendation. Students aged 14 and 16, who slept for a median of 8 and 7.5 hours respectively, likewise did not achieve optimal sleep length, which for adolescents aged 10–17 is recommended to be 8.5–9.25 hours per night (Carskadon and Acebo 2002). Children's sleep periods were around 30–40 minutes shorter in our study than in a previous study by Klackenberg (1982) with children born in the 1950s. Studies show that adults today have a shorter period of sleep, and the same seems to apply in our children. It is important to point out that our study is based on a subjective evaluation of sleep periods; we have not conducted any objective measurements using EEG or actigraphy, for example. The youngest students went to bed at 8 p.m. and the eldest at 11 p.m. In my school health office, I have an old poster showing a mother saying goodnight to her children after tucking them into bed. The clock shows a time of 7 p.m. And these were school-age children!

In survey II, carried out among 204 students aged 16 in 2013, the median sleep length was one half hour longer than in survey I, carried out in 2008-2009. The median bedtime on weeknights was one half hour earlier as well in survey II. We do not have any explanation for this fact, but the hypothesis is that this falls within the margin of error.

Table 6. Checking Facebook or social media more than 10 times a day
(n=204)

	Checking Facebook or social media more than 10 times a day n=55 (27%)	Checking Facebook or social media less than 10 times a day n=149 (73%)	P value[a]
Tired in school	35 (64%)	62 (42%)	0.010*
Difficulties falling asleep	16 (29%)	24 (16%)	0.049*
Difficulties waking up	38 (69%)	84 (56%)	0.172
Enjoying school very much	30 (55%)	94 (63%)	0.056
Short sleep (less than 8 h)	27 (49%)	43 (29%)	0.011*
Late bedtime on weeknights (after 10:30 p.m.)	27 (49%)	44 (30%)	0.016*
Waking up late on weekends (after 10 a.m.)	25 (45%)	53 (36%)	0.211
Late bedtime on weekends (after 12 a.m.)	29 (53%)	62 (21%)	0.223
Being female	26 (47%)	45 (30%)	0.046*

[a]Chi-square test.

Table 5. Factors associated with sending or receiving text messages at night at least once a week (n=204) in the logistic regression analysis carried out

Variables	Odds ratio	95% CI for OR	P values
Tired in school	0.828	0.322-2.132	0.696
Difficulties falling asleep	0.935	0.318-2.749	0.935
Difficulties waking up	2.663	0.933-7.602	0.067
Enjoying school very much	1.834	0.740-4.542	0.190
Short sleep (less than 8 h)	2.228	0.740-6.704	0.154
Late bedtime on weeknights (after 10:30 p.m.)	0.578	0.187-1.792	0.343
Waking up late on weekends (after 10 p.m.)	1.229	0.476-3.169	0.670
Late bedtime on weekends (after 12 a.m.)	4.683	1.677-13.080	0.003*
Checking Facebook or social media >10 times a day	4.156	1.674-10.313	0.002*
Being female	1.550	1.128-2.130	0.007*

Note: Hosmer and Lemeshow goodness-of-fit test, p= 0.101. Nagelkerke R^2= 0.348.

Texting at night is a sleep disturbing activity. Sending or receiving text messages at night was associated with late bedtimes on weekends and often checking Facebook or other social media sites. It was also significantly more common in individuals with short sleep, with irregular sleep patterns (i.e., differences between weeknights and weekends), having sleep problems, and enjoying school to a lesser extent.

Frequent checking of Facebook or other social media sites (>10 times a day) seems to be negatively related to sleep problems. In survey II, adolescents who reported checking Facebook or other social media sites more than 10 times a day significantly more often had short sleep and difficulties falling asleep, were often tired in school, and went to bed later on weeknights. However, in a cross-sectional study, it is not possible to draw conclusions about causality. Individuals with sleep problems might use social media and texting more frequently because of their problems.

Fact box 1. How to fight sleep disruption

Is there sufficient motivation?
Sleep journal
Parental involvement
Media habits (TV, computers, mobile phone). Avoid TV in your room.
Outdoors, 1 hour a day
Training, when?
Coffee/alcohol/tobacco/energy drinks
Regularity (even weekends...) Strict wake-up times.
Hot footbath in the evening (affects distal skin blood flow)
Hope and patience!

IMPLICATIONS FOR PRACTICE

To start off, it must be stressed that there are rarely any simple solutions. My primary piece of advice is to be patient and instil hope in the children/adolescents and their families. There are many different ways to tackle the problem and they usually work. Motivational talks are often effective in these situations (Miller et al., 2008). Begin by asking the child what motivation he/she has for sleeping better, going to bed earlier, not skipping school or whatever the problem may be. A student who, for example, has made every effort to stay up until 2 a.m. and is proud of it is probably not very motivated to go to bed early. One effective way of determining sleeping habits is to ask the children to keep a sleep journal. This is usually a good way for the family to become aware of the problem, and sometimes you may discover that there *is* no problem, or it is not as serious as initially anticipated. As is usually the case, parental involvement is a common success factor. Make it clear to your children that you make the rules about bedtime and TV/computer times. Tell them that sleep disruption is more common among students with TV in their rooms and those with long 'screen times'. Mobile phones are another common disruptive element for many teenagers. Tell the teenager about the different stages of sleep, what happens where we are woken from a deep sleep by an SMS alert and how long it takes for the body to return to the all-important deep sleep. Talk about the importance of daylight for a good melatonin balance. It is easier to sleep when we have high content of melatonin in the body, but that only occurs if the body is exposed to plenty of daylight during the day and darkness at night time. A good exercise could be to make sure your children go outdoors for one hour a day. Although training is good for your health and sleep, it can sometimes be difficult to wind down directly after training. Doing ten push-ups delays sleep by one hour. Ask them if they drink coffee, cola, energy drinks or alcohol or use tobacco and tell them about these substances' negative effects on sleep. Perhaps the most important (but perhaps also the most boring) piece of advice concerns regularity. It is important to be disciplined and keep strict wake-up times, even at weekends, if you have a sleep problem.

CONCLUSION

Children who slept less than the median length of time reported enjoying school to a lesser degree. Fewer hours of sleep were found to be associated with having a bedroom television, using the television or computer more than 2 hours a day, being tired at school, and having difficulties in sleeping and waking up. Overweight and obesity were found in 15.8% of the study population; obesity alone was found in 3.1%. Relationships between lifestyle factors and overweight were studied using multivariate logistic regression analysis. Having a bedroom television and using the television more than 2 hours per day were found to be associated with overweight, but using the computer more than 2 hours a day was not. About 61% of the students aged 16 reported checking Facebook or social media at least once a day, and 27% reported doing so more than 10 times a day. One fourth of the students aged 16 had a habit of sending or receiving text messages at night at least once a week. Texting at night, and frequent checking of Facebook and social media sites were related to sleep problems. Educating schoolchildren and their parents regarding matters of optimal sleep and how media habits affect sleep, overweight and learning is considered an important task.

ACKNOWLEDGMENTS

I am grateful to the students and the school nurses who participated for their efforts and their kind cooperation in connection with the study. The study was supported by Södra Sveriges Sjuksköterskehem SSSH, the Queen Silvia Jubilee Fund, the Fanny Ekdahl Foundation for Paediatric Research, the Swedish Insurance Society, the Ebba Danelius Foundation (of the Swedish

Society of Nursing), the Kempe-Carlgrenska Foundation, and the Swedish Sleep Research Society.

REFERENCES

Adolphus K, Lawton CL, Dye L (2013). The effects of breakfast on behavior and academic performance in children and adolescents. *Front Hum Neurosci.* 8 (7), 425.

American Academy of Pediatrics (2001). Children, adolescents, and television. *Pediatrics* 107 (2), 423-6.

Carskadon MA, Acebo C (2002). Regulation of sleepiness in adolescents: Update, insights, and speculation. *Sleep* 25, 606-14.

Cole TJ, Bellizzi MC, Flegal KM, Dietz WH (2000). Establishing a standard definition for child overweight and obesity worldwide: international survey. *BMJ* 320, 1240-43.

Garmy P, Jakobsson U, Nyberg P (2012[a]). Development and psychometric evaluation of a new instrument for measuring sleep length and television and computer habits in Swedish school-age children. *Journal of School Nursing* 28, 138-143.

Garmy P, Nyberg P, Jakobsson U (2012[b]). Sleep and television and computer habits of Swedish school-age children. *Journal of School Nursing* 28, 469-76.

Garmy P, Clausson E, Nyberg P, Jakobsson U (2013). Overweight and television and computer habits in Swedish school-age children and adolescents: A cross-sectional study. *Nursing and Health Sciences* Jun 25. doi: 10.1111/nhs.12076. [Epub ahead of print].

Gregory AM, Van der Ende J, Willis TA, Verhulst FC (2008). Parent-reported sleep problems during development and self-reported anxiety/depression, attention problems, and aggressive behavior later in life. *Arch Pediatr Adolesc Med.*,162 (4), 330-5.

Klackenberg G (1982). Sleep behavior studied longitudinally. *Acta Peadiatrica Scandinavia,* 71, 501-6.

Kryger MH, Dement W, Roth T (2011). *Principle and Practice of Sleep Medicine* 5th ed. Philadelphia, PA: Elsevier Saunders.

Lager AC, Fossum B, Rörvall G, Bremberg SG (2009) Children's overweight and obesity: local and national monitoring using electronic health records. *Scand J. Public Health* 37, 201-5.

Miller WR, Rollnik S, Butler C (2008). Motivational interviewing in health care. Helping people change behavior. New York, NY: Guilford Press.

Norman GR, Streiner DL (2008) *Biostatistics the bare essentials* 3rd ed. Hamilton, ON: BC Decker Inc.

Sjöberg A, Lissner L, Albertsson-Wikland K, Mårlid S (2008). Recent anthropometric trends among Swedish school children: evidence for decreasing prevalence of overweight in girls. *Acta Paediatr* 97, 118-23.

Sjöberg A, Moreaus L, Yngve A, Poortvliet E, Al-Ansari U, Lissner L (2011). Overweight and obesity in a representative sample of school-children – exploring the urban-rural gradient in Sweden. *Obes. Rev.* 12, 305-14.

Sundblom E, Petzold M, Rasmussen F, Callmer E, Lissner L (2008). Childhood overweight and obesity prevalence leveling off in Stockholm but socioeconomic differences persist. *Int J. Obes.* 32, 1525-30.

Spruyt K, Molfese DL, Gozal D. (2011) .Sleep duration, sleep regularity, body weight, and metabolic homeostasis in school-aged children. *Pediatrics* 2011 Feb;127(2), e345-52.

Wahlstrom K (2010). School Start Time and Sleepy Teens. *Arch Pediatr Adolesc Med.* 164(7), 676-7.

In: Psychology of Habits
Editor: Robin Mazzariello

ISBN: 978-1-62948-959-9
© 2014 Nova Science Publishers, Inc.

Chapter 3

PSYCHOLOGY OF HOLY FOOD HABITS, FEAST AND FAST, IN INDOCHINA CONTEXT

Beuy Joob[1] and Viroj Wiwanitkit[2]

[1]Sanitation 1 Medical Academic Center
[2]Visiting Professor, Hainan Medical University, China
Visiting professor, Faculty of Medicine,
University of Nis, Serbia

ABSTRACT

An important consideration in clinical nutrition management is food habits. The psychology of food habits is very interesting and can be useful for management of nutritional problem. Sometimes, the spiritual aspect of food habits play important role as determinant of final overt food habits. The holy food habits must be well explored and understood by practitioner. The important habits on holy feast and holy fast are the general appearances in many communities, especially those in developing countries. In this article, the authors briefly review and discuss on Psychology of holy food habits, feast and fast, in Indochina, a developing region of the world at present, context.

INTRODUCTION

The belief is usually relating to the rooted culture of a community. This is a very complex issue in psychology. The common form of belief that can be seen around the world is the ritual belief relating to religious background. There are many religious practices around the world. Some are very interesting. It should be noted that the psychological aspect underlying those believes is very interesting. Of several religious and culture bound believer, the food habits should be mentioned. The holy food habits is specific habits that has many interesting issues in psychology. The holy food habits can be in either holy feast or holy fast. The impact of those described food habit in clinical medicine is a topic for further discussed.

Talking about the food and behavior, the food habits should be discussed. An important consideration in clinical nutrition management is food habits. The psychology of food habits is very interesting and can be useful for management of nutritional problem. Sometimes, the spiritual aspect of food habits play important role as determinant of final overt food habits. As already mentioned, the holy food habits has its background on spiritual dimension that has many interesting issued for further studies [1]. In fact, the holy food habits must be well explored and understood by practitioner. The important habits on holy feast and holy fast are the general appearances in many communities, especially those in developing countries. In this article, the authors briefly review and discuss on Psychology of holy food habits, feast and fast, in Indochina, a developing region of the world at present, context.

HOLY FOOD HABITS IN PRESENT MEDICINE

Holy food habits is an actual culture bound behavior. There are some reports on the spiritual dimension of this practice [1]. Also, there are other reports on physical aspects. Most studies are usually on the holy fast. First, the impact of Greek Orthodox Christian Church fasting is well-known holy food habits. Sarri et al., studied on this specific habits and concluded that the "Orthodox Christian dietary regulations are an important component of the Mediterranean diet of Crete characterised by low levels of dietary saturated fatty acids, high levels of fibre and folate, and a high consumption of fruit, vegetables and legumes [2]." Sarri et al., also found that this practice results in "a reduction in the blood lipid profile including a non-significant reduction in

HDL cholesterol and possible impact on obesity [3]." The similar finding was also reported by Papadaki et al. [4]. However, it is noted for Greek Orthodox Christian Church fasting null effect of on the blood pressure [5].

Another well-known holy fast practice is the Islamic Rahmandan practice. Ramadan is one of the five pillars of Islam and the Rahmadan month is a holy month for Muslims [6]. During this month, a duty to fast every day from sunrise to sunset must be practiced by Muslims [6]. There are many reports on the health effects of this holy habits. There are many concerns on nutritional management for the ones who practice this behavior. Most concerns in on diabetes mellitus [6]. For diabetic patients, it is noted that "close monitoring is essential to prevent complications for safe Ramadan [7]." The studies are required to further better understand on this holy habits to find the proper clinical nutritional management [8].

Holy Food Habits, Feast and Fast, in Indochina Context and Its Psychological Concern

The holy food habits can be seen in any communities around the world. While there are many reports on the holy food habits in the Western, the stories from the Eastern is usually inadequate. Due to long history of the Eastern, there are many holy food habits that are still presently little known. Here, the author will specifically discussed on the issues in Indochina context. Indochina is a specific region of the world in Southeast Asia. This area comprised of countries between India and China, covering Thailand, Malaysia, Myanmar, Cambodia, Loas and Vietnam. The specific concern on holy food habits in this area is very interesting.

A. Holy Fast

The holy fast can also be seen in Southeast Asia. First, the practice of holy fast in Ramadan month can still be seen in Muslims in this area [9 - 10]. There is an interesting study on psychological aspect of Ramadan practice from Malaysia [11]. In that work, Roy et al., studied on "experiences and self-regulation during Ramadan fasting among elite archers" and reported that "experiences associated with physical, emotional, behavioral, and spiritual dimensions dominated in the first phase of fasting, while the mental dimension surfaced increasingly in the latter phase of fasting [11]." Another study from Thailand also mentioned for long term planning for support the religious practice of Muslims including Ramadan fast to empower the youths in Islamic communities since it is an important factor determining stress management behaviors [12].

Apart from Ramadan fast, the strict Chinese vegetarianism is another interesting holy fast. This practice can be seen in some specific communities. This practice is sometimes used by specific group of patients aiming at therapeutic alternative. Recently, Supoken et al., studied on diet modifications of patients with gynecological cancer in Thailand and reported that 11 % of the patients practice Chinese vegetarianism. Supoken et al., also reported that most patients usually had diet modification accompanied with Buddhist praying [13]. This can clearly show that the holy fast is used as both physical and psychological support to the patients [13]. The use of holy fast practice and meditation seems to be the interesting issue for further psychological medicine research [14].

B. Holy Feast

The holy feast is less common than holy fast. However, it can still be seen in Southeast Asia. The Muslims who practice Ramadan fast usually practice Id el-Adhha feast. However, there is no report on this issue from Southeast Asia. Indeed, there are many forms of holy feast in many rural communities in this area. The practice is usually bounded to ghost-belief. In Thailand, ghost-belief is proposed as "religious rituals, as in the context of Thai Buddhism, provide an alternative method of dealing with grief [15]." In remote Thai communities, there is a festival called "Liang Pi" with is a Thai term meaning feeding ghost, which is a holy feast practice. The fresh meat is usually prepared and ingested. Sometimes, the practice transforms into abnormal psychological presentation of the patient. The good example is "Phii pob" which is a specific local form of spirit possession [16].

REFERENCES

[1]   Imfeld A. The spiritual dimension. From holy food habits, fasting and starvation to eating without limits measure. *Krankenpfl Soins Infirm.* 2001 Jan;94(1):12-4.

[2]   Sarri KO, Linardakis MK, Bervanaki FN, Tzanakis NE, Kafatos AG. Greek Orthodox fasting rituals: a hidden characteristic of the Mediterranean diet of Crete. *Br J Nutr.* 2004 Aug;92(2):277-84.

[3]   Sarri KO, Tzanakis NE, Linardakis MK, Mamalakis GD, Kafatos AG. Effects of Greek Orthodox Christian Church fasting on serum lipids and obesity. *BMC Public Health.* 2003 May 16;3:16.

[4]   Papadaki A, Vardavas C, Hatzis C, Kafatos A. Calcium, nutrient and food intake of Greek Orthodox Christian monks during a fasting and non-fasting week. *Public Health Nutr.* 2008 Oct;11(10):1022-9.

[5]   Sarri K, Linardakis M, Codrington C, Kafatos A. Does the periodic vegetarianism of Greek Orthodox Christians benefit blood pressure? *Prev Med.* 2007 Apr;44(4):341-8.

[6]   Zantar A, Azzoug S, Belhimer F, Chentli F. Diabetes and Ramadan. *Presse Med.* 2012 Nov;41(11):1084-8.

[7]   Fariduddin M, Mahtab H, Latif ZA, Siddiqui NI. Practical management of diabetes during Ramadan fasting. *Mymensingh Med J.* 2011 Jul;20(3):541-6.

[8]   Anson O, Anson J. Surviving the holidays: gender differences in mortality in the context of three Moslem holidays. *Sex Roles.* 1997 Sep;37(5-6):381-99.

[9]   Chongsuvivatwong V, Mo-Suwan L, Mahahing P. Transitional society, health status and international migration of Muslim villagers in the lower part of southern Thailand. *Southeast Asian J Trop Med Public Health.* 1990 Sep;21(3):442-6.

[10]   Velayudhan M. Managing diabetes during the Muslim fasting month of Ramadan. *Med. J. Malaysia.* 2012 Jun;67(3):353-4.

[11]   Roy J, Hamidan S, Singh R. Temporal Patterns of Subjective Experiences and Self-Regulation during Ramadan Fasting among Elite Archers: A Qualitative Analysis. *Asian J. Sports Med.* 2011 Sep;2 (3):195-204.

[12]   Jaeasae R, Suthirangsri W, Lertpaiboon J. Factors influencing stress management behaviors of Thai Muslim High-School adolescents in three border provinces of Southern Thailand. *J. Ment Health Thai.* 2005; 13(2): 68-77.

[13]   Supoken A, Chaisrisawatsuk T, Chumworathayi B. Proportion of gynecologic cancer patients using complementary and alternative medicine. *Asian Pac. J. Cancer Prev.* 2009;10(5):779-82.

[14]   Rozenberg G. Vegetarianism and holiness in Theravada Buddhism: rereading ancient sources in the light of contemporary reality. *Arch. Sci. Soc Relig.* 2002;47(120):5-31.

[15] Sorajjakool S. Tsunami and ghost stories in Thailand: exploring the
      psychology of ghosts and religious rituals within the context of Thai
      Buddhism. *J. Pastoral Care Counsel.* 2007 Winter;61(4):343-9.
[16] Suwanlert S. Phii pob and spirit possession: the psychiatrist's point of
      view. *Psychiatr Assoc. Thai.* 2000; 45(4): 301-310.

In: Psychology of Habits
Editor: Robin Mazzariello

Chapter 4

DISORDERED EATING HABITS AMONG ADOLESCENTS

Patricia Mawusi Amos[1], Freda Dzifa Intiful[2],
Theresa Antwi[1], Christina Ammah[1]
and Ruth Adisetu Pobee[3]*

[1]University of Education, Winneba; Ghana
[2]University of Ghana, Legon, Ghana
[3]Food Research Institute, Ghana

ABSTRACT

Disordered eating habits among adolescents remains a major global problem that can affect their physical, mental and behavioral development. In spite of the advances that have been made in feeding practices, adolescents in many environments consume diets that are nutritionally inadequate, in that they do not provide adequate amounts of essential nutrients. Adolescence is a period which is critical and characterized by various growth spurts. Some of these growth spurts are psychological and emotional. Good dietary habits have also been found to be crucial in the development and growth of the adolescent during these periods. These psychological and emotional changes can lead to eating disorders if not well attended to. The three main types of disordered eating habits that can affect adolescents are anorexia nervosa, bulimia

---

* Corresponding Authors Email: pathogrey@gmail.com.

nervosa and binge eating disorder. In this review the use of a multidisciplinary approach in ensuring optimum adolescent growth was addressed. This approach included the use of parents/care-takers, teachers, dieticians, clinical psychologists and counsellors to ensure healthy eating habits of some adolescents. The results indicated the invaluable contribution of all the stakeholders in achieving good nutrition among adolescents.

I. ADOLESCENCE: PSYCHOLOGICAL AND EMOTIONAL CHANGES DURING ADOLESCENCE

Definition of Adolescence

Adolescence describes the teenage years between 13 and 19 and can be considered the transitional stage from childhood to adulthood. However, the physical, emotional and psychological changes that occur in adolescence can start earlier, during the pre-teen years (ages 9-12) [Santrock, 2005].

A thorough understanding of adolescence in society depends on information from various perspectives, most importantly from the areas of Psychology, Biology, History, Sociology, Education and Anthropology. Within all of these perspectives, adolescence is viewed as a transitional period between childhood and adulthood, whose cultural purpose is the preparation of children for adult roles. It is a period of multiple transitions involving education, training, employment and unemployment, as well as transitions from one living circumstance to another (Larson & Wilson, 2004). The adolescent period is characterised by critical periods which may have negative influence on their lives. One main issue is their eating habits, which if not well checked can be disordered. In discussing adolescent eating disorders it will be expedient to have a brief description of the various changes that occur during this critical period.

Physiological and Physical Changes in Adolescents

Some of the most significant parts of adolescent development involve distinctive physiological and physical changes in individuals' height, weight, body composition, circulatory and respiratory systems. These changes are largely influenced by hormonal activity. Hormones play an organizational role, priming the body to behave in a certain way once puberty begins. Hormones also play an active role, which refers to changes in hormones during adolescence that trigger behavioural and physical changes (Sisk & Foster, 2004; Simmons & Blyth, 1987).

Adolescence is the stage of life in which children develop secondary sex characteristics (for example, a deeper voice and larger Adams's apple in boys, and development of breast and more curved and prominent hips in girls) as their hormonal balance shifts strongly towards an adult state. This is triggered by the pituitary gland, which secretes a surge of hormonal agents into the blood stream, initiating a chain reaction. The male and female gonads are subsequently activated, which puts them into a state of rapid growth and development; the triggered gonads now commence the mass production of the necessary chemicals. The testes primarily release testosterone, and the ovaries predominantly dispense oestrogens. The production of these hormones increases gradually until sexual maturation is met. Some boys may develop gynaecomastia due to an imbalance of sex hormones, tissue responsiveness and obesity (Slap & Gail, 2001)

Another set of significant physical changes during puberty for males is the first ejaculation, which occurs, on average, at age 13. Females, it is menarche, the onset of menstruation, which occurs, on average, between ages 12 and 13 (Al-Sahab, Ardern, Hamadeh & Tamim, 2010). The age of menarche is influenced by heredity, but a girl's diet and lifestyle may also contribute. Regardless of genes, a girl must have a certain proportion of body fat to attain menarche.

Another set of significant physical changes during puberty for adolescents is eating disorders. Eating disorders happen as a result of severe disturbances in eating behaviour, such as unhealthy reduction of food intake or extreme overeating. These patterns can be caused by feelings of distress or concern about body shape or weight and they harm normal body composition and function. A person with an eating disorder may have started out just eating smaller or larger amounts of food than usual, but at some point, the urge to eat less or more spirals out of control.

Eating disorders are very complex, and despite scientific research to understand them, the biological, behavioural and social underpinnings of these illnesses remain elusive. Eating disorders frequently develop during adolescence or early adulthood, but some reports indicate their onset can occur during childhood or later in adulthood. Although studies have shown that, childhood experiences with food plays an important role in eating habits later in life, it can be clearly seen during the adolescents' physical changes.

Many adolescents not only express dissatisfaction with their figure, shape and weight, but also exhibit disordered eating behaviour, such as binge eating (eating a large amount of food with a sense of lack of control), food restriction, laxative abuse and vomiting. In a Minnesota school-based survey with more than 80,000 participants, 56% of the 9th grade females and 28% of the 9th-grade males reported disordered eating behaviours such as fasting, vomiting or binge eating; in the 12th-grade females and males, slightly higher rates of 57% and 31%, respectively, were found (Croll, Neumark-Sztainer, Story & Ireland, 2002).

In a North Italian study, 28% of 15 to 19-year-old female high school adolescents reported unhealthy eating behaviours as described earlier. Also, nearly half of all American high school girls diet to lose weight through disordered eating habits when they reach sexual maturation (Toselli et al., 2005).

In general, girls report more disordered eating and body image concerns than boys, and youngsters of higher grades are more vulnerable than those of lower grades. In contrast to former assumptions, eating disorder issues are not exclusively found in underweight females, but also in overweight adolescents of both sexes (Poskitt, 1995).

Emotional and Psychological Changes

The physical changes associated with puberty become the basis for new emotional and psychological experiences. Besides the many physical changes that occur during puberty, many emotional and psychological changes take place as well. Emotion is a feeling or an effect that involves physiological arousal, behavioural expression and sometimes conscious experiences, whilst psychology is how the mind influences behaviour in a particular way of life. Relationships with others may begin to change as well as their eating habits. Adolescents begin to separate more from parents and identify with other peers of the same age. They begin to feel self-conscious about their bodies and the way they look. Comparisons begin with self and other peers (Santrock, 2005). One must remember that everyone goes through puberty at a different pace and eventually, everyone catches up. During this time, adolescents also become more aware of their sexuality (Harden & Mendle, 2011).

Emotional and psychological changes that occur during adolescents include the following:

- **Feeling overly sensitive**

The adolescence body undergoes many changes as such; there is extreme sensitivity during the adolescents' stage. During this period, they feel uncomfortable about themselves and as a result they may be irritated quite easily, lose their temper or feel depressed over trivial issues (Simmons & Blyth, 1987). Depression and anxiety during adolescents as emotional and psychological change include problematic eating behaviours such as "mindless eating," frequent snacking on high-calorie foods, overeating and night eating, where the majority of adolescents with binge eating disorder become overweight (Glinski, Wetzler & Goodman, 2001).

- **Mood swings**

To add to the uncertainty and conflicting thoughts, adolescence may also experience frequent and sometimes extreme changes in their mood. Their mood will swing between feeling confident and happy to feeling irritated and depressed in a short span of time. These frequent swings about how they feel are called "mood swings". These changes in moods may occur due to shifting levels of hormones in their blood for example, estrogen and testosterone levels in girls' and boys' respectively.

In Ghana for example, it is commonly observed that adolescents' eating habits become disordered during their mood swings. Majority of them tend to eat more during their happy moments and eat less (or not at all) during their sad moments or when they are stressed up.

Food is often used as a coping mechanism by adolescents with weight problems, particularly when they are sad, anxious, stressed, lonely, and frustrated. In many obese individuals there appears to be a perpetual cycle of mood disturbance, overeating, and weight gain. When they feel distressed, they turn to feed to help cope, and though such comfort eating may result in temporary attenuation of their distressed mood, the weight gain that results may cause a dysphoric mood due to their inability to control their stress.

- **Peer Influence**

The relationships adolescents have with their peers, family and members of their social sphere play a vital role in their social development. They tend to stick to their peers more than any other group in the social sphere and this usually leads to extreme peer influence over the individual. The peers begin to help the adolescent understand the concept of personalities, how they are formed and why a person has that specific type of personality. This is the first time individuals can truly make their own decisions, thus making this a sensitive period (Hundleby & Mercer, 1987; Mason, Cauce, Gonzales & Hiraga, 1994).

Peer groups are especially important during adolescence, a period of development characterized by a dramatic increase in time spent with peers and a decrease in adult supervision. Adolescents also associate with friends of the opposite sex much more than in childhood and tend to identify with larger groups of peers based on shared characteristics. It is also common for adolescents to use friends as coping devices in different situations (Larson & Richards, 1991).

Peer groups offer members the opportunity to develop social skills such as empathy, sharing and leadership. Peer groups can have positive influences on an individual, such as on academic motivation and performance. There is also attachment to a particular friend and hero worship. Their conversations with their friends will increase. They are likely to be influenced by what they see around them in popular media and the culture that is represented through them. But they can also have negative influences, like encouraging experimentation with drugs, drinking, vandalism, disordered eating habit and stealing through peer pressure. Susceptibility to peer pressure increases during early adolescence, peaks around age 14, and declines thereafter (Steinberg & Monahan, 2007).

- **Conflicting thoughts**

Confusion is heightened by the fact that in our culture one has the right to develop as an individual so long as other individuals are not jeopardized. The social confusion makes the adolescent seek answers outside himself or herself in his family group and outside world. The rules of living he or she gets are not without contradiction. There are no rigid prescriptions or guides. Adolescents' behaviour is unpredictable because it is determined by the confusion in them.

In Ghana, many traditional people hold a collectivistic cultural tradition; most families learn to conform as interdependent whole rather than independent beings. This dependency starts in the family where a parent to child hierarchy is enforced and children are taught to be submissive and obedient. This can cause rebellion in the adolescent and some of them may turn to abnormal behaviours where eating disorderly is an example. In this case, the child may want to have some control while at the same time may not want to disrespect their parents. As a result, the adolescents may not eat from home but from their own savings or depend on their friends for food. In some cases the parents as a sign of punishment to their disrespectful adolescents will not provide food for them. This may affect their eating habits as they will depend on their peers for food by sharing or perhaps buy any kind of food to eat if they have enough money with them without necessarily considering the time to eat and whether they are balanced or not.

This support the idea that loyalty versus independence played conflicting role that lead to eating disorder symptoms (Schmidt, 1993).

- **Looking for an identity and Feeling conscious about self**

Unlike the conflicting aspects of self-concept, identity represents a coherent sense of self stable across circumstances and including past experiences and future goals. Everyone has a self-concept, whereas Erik Erikson argued that not everyone fully achieves identity. Erikson's theory of stages of development includes the identity crisis in which adolescents must explore different possibilities and integrate different parts of themselves before committing to their beliefs. He described the resolution of this process as a stage of "identity achievement" but also stressed that the identity challenge "is never fully resolved once and for all at one point in time" (Steinberg, 2008).

Disordered eating habits do really impact on adolescents to explore their new identities. High self esteem is associated with under-weight in girls, this is because the adolescent girl attempt to restrict eating to obtain weight control so as to look attractive to the opposite sex.

Low self esteem is also associated with overweight in boys as well as girls and this is because adolescent boys need to build their muscles to attain slender and muscular bodies through extreme weight control behaviour such as over exercise, over eating and steroid use to obtain their standards of male beauty (Keel & Gravener, 2008).

- **Getting sexual feelings**

Sexual maturity is the stage of adolescent's life when they can have children. One aspect of sexual maturity is being curious about sex and also about bodies of people that they are attracted to. With the onset of puberty, it is normal for a boy or a girl to be sexually attracted to people that they would want to be more than 'just friends' with. The onset of sex drive and sexual desire for the opposite sex becomes very strong. American high school girls, nearly half of them diet to lose weight through disordered eating habits when they reach sexual maturation (Toselli et al., 2005).

- **Enjoyment and Entertainment**

At this stage in life, the boy or girl now feels that he or she is of age and can now enjoy life to its maximum. Many will like to be associated with well-known people, the big boys and big girls of their time. Many can outwit their parent to attend parties, beach bashes and excursions. They are not too bothered about the negative outcomes of their actions and inactions.

Eating behaviours are associated with other activities. The behaviours become conditioned to occur together, as when a person eats while watching Television. If these two behaviours are paired repeatedly, they become so strongly associated with one another that turning on the Television alone triggers a craving for food (Becker, 2004).

In the Ghanaian community most of the adolescents eating habits become affected especially in their joyous mood and during festivities. They tend to celebrate their long happy moments with food and drinks. They usually end up in overeating and weight gain. For example, most of the festive occasions in Ghana are accompanied with eating and drinking spree, where people will cook different kinds of dishes and will share freely with every individual who is willing to eat. Most adolescents take advantage of eating disorderedly from both known and unknown quarters and hence gain more weight. It is a well-known custom in the Ghanaian community to cherish people who have gained more weight. They see it as a sign of good living, and as such adolescents who gain weight during these festive occasions will continue to eat more disorderedly in order to gain more weight. Adolescents who are enlightened and are exposed to other foreign cultures tend to reduce the amount of food they take in order not to gain weight.

All the emotional, physiological and psychological changes discussed one way or the other have some effect on the eating habits of adolescents in that these changes may influence their eating habits.

II. WHAT ARE DISORDERED EATING HABITS?

Disordered eating habits as defined by Mahan & Escott-Stump (2008) is the abnormal behavior related to food and eating which may include starving, binging, vomiting, laxative abuse or excessive exercise accompanied by unrealistic ideas about food, a distorted body image and psychological and developmental abnormalities. The American Psychiatric Association has classified disordered eating habits into anorexia nervosa, bulimia nervosa, and binge eating.

Anorexia nervosa is characterized by the refusal of the individual to maintain body weight at or above a minimally normal weight for age and height. Also even though the individual is seen by others as being underweight, the individual fears she would gain weight if she eats even though in actual fact she is underweight. Accompanying these symptoms may be amenorrhoea.

Bulimia nervosa is also usually characterized by periodic episodes of binge eating. Also accompanying the binge eating, the individual could indulge herself in some isolated periods of eating. In addition to these habits, the individual may feel a sense of lack of control over eating during the periods of binging. After the consumption, the person would also indulge in compensatory behavior that is intended to prevent weight gain. Such behaviours involve excessive exercise, laxative use, induced vomiting and diuretic use.

Binge eating is also considered as a disordered eating habit. Individuals involved in binge eating binge on food. However they do not indulge in compensatory behaviours such as induced vomiting, excessive exercise and laxative use.

III. PSYCHOLOGY OF DISORDERED EATING

Eating has been an important issue in the field of psychology. This is due to the fact that numerous disorders or problems are linked to eating and these problems can result in severe disorders whereby the types of eating disorders are not exception. In fact psychology of eating has been an essential field of study in this century. Since adolescence is a critical stage, it is necessary for caretakers and parents to ensure that they take well-nourished food to facilitate their normal growth and development. It should be noted that adolescents' food intake and nutrition must be monitored regularly and ordered according to their growing needs.

Sadness and happiness can influence eating. Emotionally when one feels sad, he or she may resort to eating. It is not different when one feels happy too. Occasionally, friends and loved ones when they meet use food as a way of showing their joy for meeting each other. So after exchanging pleasantries for some time; resort to food to express their satisfaction in meeting each other. In some countries, a funeral which is believed to be a sad moment is not so different from parties. It is expected that the deceased family will refresh sympathisers with drinks and food to show their appreciation.

In the same vein Questia. Com (2013) research revealed that memory and learning also play an essential role in eating behaviours. The taste of a food whether good or bad when memorised can determine how much one will eat in the next meal. Again, how people see foods being mishandled especially animal foods, emotionally and psychologically become resilient to it. For example during childhood when one finds food unpleasant, Questia.com noted that such individuals may reject it during adulthood.

IV. CAUSES AND EFFECTS OF DISORDERED EATING HABITS

Eating habits are developed over a period of time. They do not happen in a day. Many factors interact with each other to form an individual's eating habit. Various factors contribute to good or poor eating habits. The factors that contribute to the development of good eating habits may be the same that may contribute to disordered eating depending on whether the factors produced positive or negative tendencies. Polivy & Herman, (2002) describes some factors that can contribute to the formation of disordered eating habits.

The first and foremost factor that has to be addressed is the sociocultural factors. The culture and socioeconomic status pertaining at a particular place can influence people's eating habits. For instance in Ghana, obesity and overweight are associated with beauty and success (Amoah, 2003). This falls in line with Polivy & Herman's assertion that cultures that are faced with scarcity in food tend to adore obesity. On the other hand in cultures where there is abundance of food, slim body is idealized. Studies indicate that disordered eating is most prevalent in cultures where food is found to be in abundance. Therefore western cultures tend to have high prevalence of eating disorders compared to other cultures (Cummins & Lehman, 2007).

The media is regarded as one of the potent tools for promoting ideas. In cultivating certain eating habits, the media has been implicated. In recent times, the media tends to portray that slimness is the ideal body image that everyone should have. Therefore, adolescents tend to follow certain eating habits that can get them the body image they desire. This can lead to the cultivation of disordered eating habits. In 1996, Tiggermann and Pickering discovered that the passion for thinness among girls increased as a result of exposure to particular TV shows.

Peers have also been found to be very influential in adolescent choices and development of certain habits. The peers of adolescents have been shown to influence their eating habits. In Ghana, peers were found to be the most predictor of adolescent dietary habits (Amos, Intiful & Boateng, 2012). Some studies have cited the influence of peers as one of the major contributors to the development of bad eating habits such as eating disorders (Shisslak et al., 1998, Stice 1998, Wertheim et al., 1997). Therefore peers are considered to be contributors to development of eating disorders particularly in adolescent. This may stem from the fact that many of these adolescents want recognition from their peers and therefore would take up certain habits to be accepted by their peers.

Besides the sociocultural factors, biological and psychological factors have also been implicated to be among the causes of eating disorders. Biological factors such as genetic predisposition have been found to be linked to eating disorders. Also certain biochemical factors involving irregularities in the formation and transmission of some hormones, amino acids and homocysteine have been found to be associated with people with disordered eating habits (Chaudhri et al., 2006; Wilhelm et al., 1996).

The effects of disordered eating can be enormous if not well checked. A person with anorexia nervosa is likely to experience weakness and fainting, dryness and thinning of the hair and sometimes hair loss. Also an individual may also experience menstrual irregularities, weight loss, low blood pressure, muscle loss, severe dehydration, anaemia and hyperactivity.

Bulimia Nervosa on the other hand is characterized by the individual having a distorted body image and therefore has an obsessive desire to lose weight. In this effort to lose weight, the individual cultivates the habit of bouts of extreme overeating which is followed by fasting or self induced vomiting or purging. A person with this habit is likely to experience the following symptoms; damaged teeth and gums, peptic ulcers and pancreatitis, abnormal bowels, loss of menstruation or irregularities in menstruation, sores in the throat and mouth, eating excessively, dehydration, irregular bowel movements, constipation and swollen salivary glands.

V. TREATING DISORDERED EATING HABITS AMONG ADOLESCENTS: THE ROLE OF THE MULTIDISCIPLINARY TEAM

Eating disorders namely; Anorexia nervosa, bulimia nervosa and binge eating have multifactorial etiologies which require multidimensional approaches for effective treatment. The etiology of eating disorders can be categorized as physiological or biological vulnerability, psychological predispositions, family disturbances and sociocultural influences (Halmi, 2005). Thus the integrated effect of these challenges propels the individual person into developing an eating disorder which requires an interdisciplinary culture sensitive team such as Psychiatrists for pharmacotherapy, (Halmi, 2005), clinical psychologists for psychotherapy, nutritionists for dietary management and education, specialist physicians such as pediatricians for children below 18years, gynecologists and dentists for treatment.

It must be noted that the treatment strategy should depend on the severity of the specific eating disorder, since different disorders require different strategies as well as a culture sensitive multidisciplinary team. This is because patients requiring treatment come from different cultural backgrounds. For example the treatment of eating disorders has always seemed to focus on western philosophy which contradicts non western cultures. This is because traditionally eating disorders have been labeled as western culture bound syndromes resulting from the internalization of unhealthy thin body ideal represented western society (Goldring & Lopez, 2013), however recent studies have revealed that eating disorders are prevalent among people of non-western who have been exposed to western cultural ideals either through living in a western culture for example the Chinese Americans or living in their own culture but have western exposure for body weight and shape. Thus the ideal multidisciplinary team are likely to succeed if they make specific client cultural adaptations to their existing treatments by taking into consideration the norms, values, and expectations, religious beliefs and practices within the culture of the patient. For example non western cultures like the Chinese, Native Americans, and Latin Americans value interdependence, communalism, respect for elders, cooperation and harmony in families, thus assertive and confrontational methods of dealing with challenges in families will threaten these values and bring disharmony in the family.

Treatment of Specific Disorders

Anorexia Nervosa

The etiology and course of anorexia have been reported to be less responsive to treatment than bulimia, (Mash & Wolfe, 2013) this is because of the challenges of small sample size, unmotivated patients, complications and very few randomized controlled trials; nevertheless some inroads are being made.

Some of the elements for the treatment of this disorder according to (Halmi, 2005) are psychotherapy, psychopharmacology and nutritional rehabilitation.

Psychotherapy involves behavioral, cognitive and family therapy. Cognitive therapy for anorexia nervosa involves helping the patient to a) identify distorted thought of feeling fat, b) list the evidence for these thoughts, c) list the evidence against these thoughts, d) form a reasonable conclusion and e) use the rational conclusion to guide future behavior. Another element in cognitive therapy is monitoring. Halmi (2005), assert that monitoring involves patients making daily records of food intake, including type of food, the time of eating and the environment it occurred. It also involves records of binge/purging behavior, exercise and interpersonal difficulties (Kleifield, Wagner & Halmi, 1996).

Family therapy has also been known to be an effective form of treatment for anorexia nervosa. This involves the family members especially the parents or guardians of the patient to explore the patterns and expectations within the family that reinforce the eating disorder and to restore healthy communication patterns (Wilson, Grilo, & Vitousek 2007). Family members can be seen separately if that seem to be the best approach or all are seen at the same time that is conjoint family therapy. For example in a comparative study by Goldring & Lopez (2013), they found that family therapy for client in the USA do not necessarily require the physical presence of the parents in order to heal the relationship within the family. However in Argentina, the treatment required the physical presence of the family and on site interaction and healing.

Pharmacotherapy involves the use of antipsychotic medication to treat the disorder. Promising pilot studies of pharmacotherapy conclude that antipsychotic medications such as olanzapine and quetapine may be helpful during weight restoration phase. Citalopram may reduce depression and anxiety during weight restoration (Halmi, 2005).

Bulimia Nervosa

In contrast to anorexia nervosa, treatments of bulimia have been conducted in the past fifteen years with promising results (Halmi, 2005). Some of the main elements in the treatment of this disorder are psychotherapy, pharmacotherapy and nutritional management.

Cognitive behavioral therapy has been known to be the first choice of treatment for bulimia nervosa since it has been shown to be most effective current therapy delivered individually or by involving the family (Rutherford & Couturier; 2007; Wilson et al., 2007). Cognitive behavioral therapy change dieting behaviors rather than controlling bingeing by reinforcing desirable or appropriate behavior and by helping patients change distorted personal or socio cultural patterns of thinking that contribute to their obsession. It also addresses interpersonal issues such as distorted drive for thinness (Stic, Rohde, Shaw, & Gau, 2011). It also involves self-monitoring by which patients monitor their food intake, bingeing and purging episodes and the thoughts and feelings that trigger these episodes. This is done in combination with regular weighing, introduction of avoided food and meal planning designed to bring eating behavior back to normal.

Nutritional rehabilitation involves establishing regular patterns of non-binge meals, increasing caloric intake to correct nutritional deficiencies.

In terms of the pharmacotherapy treatment for bulimia nervosa, literature reveals that antidepressant medication in dosages similar to the treatment for depression have been shown to improve mood and preoccupation with shape and weight in about 20percent of patients; however medications like Bupropion, Trasodine and the monoamine oxidase inhibitors have unfavorable side effects in the patients (DeZwaan & Roerig 2003). Fluoxetine in a dose of 60mg/day had beneficial and favorable effects.

Binge Eating Disorder

Randomized controlled treatment trials have used the same techniques as those of bulimia nervosa. Cognitive behavioral therapy and antidepressants have been shown to be effective in treating binge eating disorder in the same way in which it has been effective for bulimia nervosa (Agras, et al., 1995). For example antidepressants such as desipramine, fluvoxamine, fluoxetine, sertraline and citalopram can reduce binge eating and weight loss in the treatment of eating disorder. Treatment duration between 6 to 12 month at a level of substantial progress before any attempt at discontinuation.

CONCLUSION

The multifactorial etiology of eating disorders requires a multidisciplinary team and multidimensional approach to treatment with consideration for the severity and specific diagnosis for the type of eating disorder. It must also be emphasized that eating disorders also have a myriad of associated forms of psychopathology.

REFERENCES

Agras, W. S., Telch, C. F., Arnow, B., Eldredge, K. L., Detzer, M. J., Henderson, J. & Marnell, M. (1995). Does interpersonal therapy help patients with binge eating disorder who fail to respond to cognitive-behavioral therapy? *Journal of Consulting & Clinical Psychology, 63,* 356–360.

Al-Sahab, B., Ardern, C. I., Hamadeh, M. J., & Tamim, H. (2010). Age at menarche in Canada; results from the National Longitudinal Survey of Children and Youth. *BMC Public Health, 10,* 736.

Amoah, A. G. B. (2003). Socio demographic variations in obesity among Ghanaians Adults. *Public Health Nutrition, (6)*8, 751-757.

Amos P. M., Intiful F. D. & Boateng L. (2012). Factors That Were Found to Influence Ghanaian Adolescents' Eating Habits. *SAGE Open* October-December 2012: 1 –6. DOI: 10.1177/2158244012468140. http://sgo. sagepub.com.

Becker, A. E. (2004). Television disordered eating and young women in Fiji: Negotiating body image and identity during rapid social change. *Culture Medicine and Psychiatry, 28,* 533-559.

Chaudhri, O., Small, C. & Bloom, S. (2006). Gastrointestinal hormones regulating appetite. *Philosophical Transactions of the Royal Society* B (361)1471, 1187–209.

Croll, J., Neumark-Sztainer, D., Story, M., & Ireland, M. (2002). Prevalence and risk and protective factors related to disordered eating behaviours among adolescents: relationship to gender and ethnicity. *J. Adolescent Health, 31,*166–175.

Cummins, L. H. & Lehman, J. (2007). 40% of eating disorder cases are diagnosed in females ages 15-19 years old (Hoe van Hoeken, 2003). Eating disorders and body image concerns in Asian American women:

Assessment and treatment from a multi-cultural and feminist perspective. *Eating Disorders, 15*, 217-230.

DeZwaan, M., & Roerig, J. (2003). Pharmacological treatment of eating disorders: a review. In: Maj M, editor; Halmi, K., editor; Lopez-Ibor, J.J., Sartorius, N. editors. *Eating disorders*. New York: J. Wiley, pp. 223–286.

Glinski, J., Wetzler, S., & Goodman, E. (2001). The psychology of gastric bypass surgery. *Obesity Surgery, 11*, 581-588.

Goldring, M. & Lopez, S. (*2013)*. The Cultural Implications of Eating Disorders: A Comparative Study Between Argentina and the United States.

Halmi, K. A. (2005).The multimodal treatment of eating disorders. *World Psychiatry. 4*(2): 69–73.

Harden, K., & Mendle, J. (2011). Adolescent sexual activity and the development of delinquent behaviour: The role of relationship context. *Journal of Youth and Adolescence, 40*(7), 825–838.

Hundleby, J. D., & Mercer, G. W. (1987). Family and friends as social environments and their relationship to young adolescents' use of alcohol, tobacco, and marijuana. *Journal of Marriage and the Family, 49*, 151-164.

Keel, P. K., & Gravener, J. A. (2008). Sociocultural influences on eating disorders. In S. Wonderlich, J. Mitchell, M. de Zwan, & H. Steiger (Eds.), *Annual review of eating disorders*, (pp. 43–57). Oxford: Radcliffe Publishing.

Kleifield, E. I., Wagner, S. & Halmi K. A. (1996). Cognitive-behavioral treatment of anorexia nervosa. *Psychiatr Clin North Am. 19*:715–734.

Larson R., & Richards M. (1991). Daily companionship in late childhood and early adolescence: Changing developmental contexts". *Child Development, 62*(2), 284–300.

Larson, R., & Wilson, S. (2004). Adolescence across place and time: Globalization and the pathways to adulthood. In R. Lerner and L. Steinberg (Eds.), Handbook of adolescent psychology. New York: Wiley.

Mahan K. L. & Escott S. (2008). Krause Food and Nutrition Therapy. International Edition, 12th Edition 11830, Westline Industrial Drive St Louis Missouri, 63146.

Mash, E. J. & Wolfe, D. A. (2013). *Abnormal child psychology (5th ed.)*. Wadsworth Publishing.

Mason, C. A., Cauce, A. M., Gonzales, N. & Hiraga, Y. (1994). Adolescent problem behaviour: The effect of peers and the moderating role of father absence and the mother–child relationship. *American Journal of Community Psychology, 22,* 723-743.

Polivy, J. & Herman, P. (2002). Causes of eating disorders. *Annual Review of Psychology, 53,* 187-213. Retrieved from http://psych.annualreviews.org.

Poskitt, E. M. E. (1995). Defining childhood obesity: the relative body mass index (BMI). Acta Paediatr, *8,* 961–963.

Questia (2013). *Psychology of eating.* Retrieved from http://www.questia.com /library/psychology/other-types-of-psychology/psychology-of-eating.

Rutherford, L. & Couturier, J. (2007). A review of psychotherapeutic interventions for Children and adolescents with eating disorders. *J Can Acad Child Adolesc Psychiatry.16*(4): 153–157.

Santrock, J. W. (2005). *Adolescent (10th Ed.).* New York: McGraw-Hill.

Schmidt, U. (1993). "Bulimia nervosa in the Chinese" *International Journal of Eating Disorders 14*(4):505-509.

Shisslak, C. M., Crago, M,. McKnight, K. M,. Estes, L. S,. Gray, N. & Parnaby, O. G. (1998). Potential risk factors associated with weight control behaviors in elementary and middle school girls. *J. Psychosom. Res. 44,* 301–13.

Simmons, R., & Blyth, D. (1987). *Moving into adolescence.* New York: Aldine de Gruyter.

Sisk, C. L., & Foster D. L. (2004). The neural basis of puberty and adolescence. *Nature Neuroscience, 7*(10), 1040–1047.

Slap, M. D., & Gail, B. (2001). *Breast Enlargement in Adolescent Boys. M.D. University of Pennsylvania School of Medicine.* Retrieved September 20, 2013 from http://www.healthline.com/galecontent/breast-enlargement-in-adolescent-boys.

Steinberg, L. (2008). *Adolescence (8th Ed.).* New York, NY: McGraw-Hill.

Steinberg, L., & Monahan, K. C. (2007). Age Differences in Resistance to Peer Influence. *Developmental psychology, 43*(6), 1531–1543.

Stice, E. (1998). Modeling of eating pathology and social reinforcement of the thin-ideal predict onset of bulimic symptoms. *Behav Res. Ther. 36,* 931–44.

Stice, E., Rohde, P., Gau, J., & Shaw, H. (2011). An effectiveness trial of a dissonance-based eating disorder prevention program for high-risk adolescents. *Journal of Consulting and Clinical Psychology,* (77)5, 825-834.

Tiggermann, P. A. S. (1996). Role of television in adolescent women's body dissatisfaction and drive for thinness. *Int. J. Eat. Disord.* 20, 199-203.

Toselli, A. L., Villani, S., Ferro, A. M., Verri, A., Cucurullo, L., & Marinoni, A. (2005). Eating disorders and their correlates in high school adolescents of Northern Italy. *Epidemiol Psichiatr Soc, 14,* 91–99.

Wertheim, E. H, Paxton, S. J. & Shurtz Muri, S. L. (1997). Where do adolescents watch their weight? An interview study examining sociocultural pressures to be thin. *J. Psycho Som. Rev. 42*, 345-355.

Wilhelm, J., Müller, E., De Zwaan, M., Fischer, J., Hillemacher, T., Kornhuber, J., Bleich, S & Frieling, H (1996). Elevation of homocysteine levels is only partially reversed after therapy in females with eating disorders. *Journal of neural transmission (Vienna, Austria : 1996)* 117 (4): 521–7.

Wilson, G.T, Grilo, C.M, & Vitousek, K.M. (2007). Psychological treatment of eating disorders. *Am Psychol. 62*(3):199-216.

INDEX

pharmacotherapy, 62, 63, 64
Philadelphia, 43
photographs, 7
physical attractiveness, 22
physicians, 62
Physiological, 52
physiological arousal, 54
pica, 3
pituitary gland, 53
platform, 7
pleasure, 22
Poland, 1, 7, 20
policy, 27
population, ix, 3, 4, 30, 33, 34, 42
positive influences, 56
preparation, 52
preservation, 6
prevention, 67
priming, 53
probability, 10
probability distribution, 10
professionals, 30
profit, 8
protective factors, 65
psychiatrist, 50
psychoactive drug, 5
psychological well-being, vii, 1
psychology, vii, ix, 45, 46, 50, 54, 59, 66, 67
psychopathology, 65
psychopharmacology, 63
psychosocial functioning, 5
psychotherapy, 62, 63, 64
puberty, 4, 20, 30, 53, 54, 57, 67
punishment, 57
P-value, 34

Q

quality of life, 5, 21
questionnaire, viii, 8, 13, 14, 29, 32, 33

R

Ramadan, 47, 48, 49
reading, 20
reality, 49
recognition, 61
recommendations, 34
recovery, 7, 20
regression, ix, 30, 34, 35, 36, 40, 42
regression analysis, ix, 30, 35, 36, 40, 42
regression model, 34
regulations, 46
rehabilitation, 63, 64
reinforcement, 67
reliability, viii, 29, 32
relief, 8
religious beliefs, 62
representativeness, 23
resolution, 57
response, 33
responsiveness, 53
restoration, 63
restrictions, 4
risk(s), 3, 5, 30, 31, 65, 67
risk factors, 67
Royal Society, 65
rules, 41, 56

S

salivary gland(s), 61
Sartorius, 66
saturated fat, 46
saturated fatty acids, 46
savings, 57
Scandinavia, 43
scarcity, 60
school, viii, 29, 31, 32, 33, 34, 35, 36, 37, 38, 39, 40, 41, 42, 43, 44, 54, 67
school work, 31
science, 33
scope, 7, 23
self esteem, 57
self-concept, 57